YOU
HAVE A
PURPOSE

BRIDGE OF HOPE

TOM VINCI

ACW Press
Nashville, TN 37222

All Scripture in this text was taken from the King James Version.

Cover Design by Alpha Advertising
Interior design by Pine Hill Graphics

Packaged by ACW Press
PO Box 110390
Nashville, TN 37222
www.acwpress.com
The views expressed or implied in this work do not necessarily reflect those of
ACW Press. Ultimate design, content, and editorial accuracy of this work is the
responsibility of the author(s).

Publisher's Cataloging-in-Publication Data
(Provided by Cassidy Cataloguing Services, Inc.)
Vinci, Tom.

    You have a purpose : bridge of hope / Tom Vinci. -- 1st ed. --
Nashville, TN : ACW Press, 2008.

        p. ; cm.

        ISBN-13: 978-1-932124-34-7
        ISBN-10: 1-932124-34-9

        1. Christian life. 2. Spiritual life--Christianity. 3. God
(Christianity)--Worship and love. 4. Stewardship, Christian.
5. Vinci, Tom. 6. Christian biography. I. Title.

BV4501.3 .V56 2007
248.4--dc22   0707

Printed in the United States of America.

Dedication

To my Lord and Savior Jesus Christ.
He is the power behind my speech,
my walk, my joy, and my life.

Acknowledgments

To my Mom and Dad who have supported me tremendously with their unconditional love.

To my loving sons Tommy and Samuel who have brought much joy into my life. They are truly a special blessing and inspiration to me.

To Minister Mary Iacobellis who has been mentoring me for over ten years.

To Laura Watson who spent countless hours editing and assisting me with this manuscript.

To the staff at ACW Press and Pine Hill Graphics for their professional guidance and superb quality.

Table of Contents

Chapter 1

Family Life

God has a purpose for every life. Even though I have had many experiences in my life, I really never knew how much God's hand was upon me and how much He loved me, until I started walking with Him in an intimate relationship.

I come from a small family–my mom, dad, brother and me. Our family lived in a lovely nine-room home, set on a hill, located on 3 1/2 acres of property. The house had a nice layout and was comfortable and cozy, even though it was spacious. The kitchen faced the east, as did the front stairwell with its many windows. There was an orange tree and a grapefruit tree in a sunny area right inside the stairwell. The living room and dining room complemented the house, with many windows as well. The grounds were beautifully landscaped with many trees and a sprawling green lawn. I remember enjoying working around the yard with my grandfather when he came over to help my dad with the yard work.

A landscape architect, my grandfather supervised and landscaped many properties over the years. He was a dedicated and skilled artist, with vast knowledge of trees, flowers, vegetables, shrubs, grading, seeding, grafting and more.

Besides his landscaping profession, my grandfather was also an avid reader. He was engrossed in reading books and magazines like the National Geographic, history books, and other informative works. He was a man filled with wisdom and understanding. I cherished all the time I spent with him doing things together. I enjoyed the stories he would share with me from his heart about when he was a little boy on their family farm.

His parents owned and operated an olive tree plantation in Italy. They also raised farm animals, and reaped the benefits of them, including fresh milk, eggs, beef, pork and poultry. I used to day-dream about being on his family's farm when I was growing up. That was my way of escaping from reality. I just loved dreaming about being in a serene environment, trying to find the peace I longed for.

My grandparents lived only two miles from us on the same street. I used to walk there after school to enjoy my grandmother's famous Italian meals. The more I ate, the better my grandmother would feel. She would always say to me, "Have some more!"

For the most part my mother was the one who managed my brother and me. I didn't have much of a relationship when I was younger with my dad, although I loved him very much. He worked hard at the office and owned his own business, with my mother assisting him.

My dad was very busy with his practice though I knew he was very dedicated to our family's welfare. Unfortunately I didn't get to see him to much during the week because he arrived home in the evenings every night. It was different with our son Tommy and me. I always had the opportunity to pick Tommy up at the bus stop, even now, I get excited. First I say, "Thank you Jesus," when Tommy's foot touches the pavement. Then I greet him, saying, "How was your day?" His answer is usually, "Good." Then he asks, "What are we doing today?" He always anticipates the best, and in turn I try to meet his needs. It is a learning experience for me to do fun stuff with my son. I thank God for my son; he is truly a gift from God.

As a child, I had many needs, and my mom was always there for me. She and I spent a lot of time together over the years. One morning I had just gotten ready to leave for school and I closed the glass storm door by pushing on it with my wrist. All of a sudden, the glass shattered into many pieces. My hand had gone right through the glass and blood started gushing all over me and every-where else. I screamed in desperation and my mom came to my rescue. She immediately washed the wound and applied a sterile dressing. Though I felt faint, she took care of me and knew exactly what to do. She encouraged me and I felt so at peace because I saw how she loved me. I felt her love and compassion. I remember how she handled everything with so much confidence and in such an orderly fashion.

I suffered another bad experience when my brother accidentally struck me in the forehead with a baseball bat, while I was attempting to be the catcher. When the bat hit me, I remember the severe pain and the bleeding, but my parents ran immediately to my aid. In both instances, I needed to go to the emergency room for stitches. There were many other needs in my life, which were always taken care of immediately by my parents. I could always count on them to care for me in a special way.

God's love was operating through my parents, yet I really wasn't aware of the depth of His presence in everyday matters. I look back and see how merciful and gracious God was then, and He has always continued to be the same loving Father. "Jesus Christ the same yesterday, and today, and for ever" (Hebrews 13:8). God has always been there for me despite the fact that I didn't spend any quality time with Him in a loving, intimate way.

My religious education started out through the years with solid teachings of the Ten Commandments. I was also taught doctrinal laws of man, which when I think about it, just added confusion to my walk with God. I have found there is only one truth when it comes to God. "Jesus saith unto him, I am the way, the truth, and the life: no man cometh unto the Father, but by me" (John 14:6). God continued to seek my heart and, with His unconditional love, responded whenever I was in need.

At times, there was a tremendous amount of fear in my life growing up. When I was ten years old, a friend of the family came over for dinner one evening and my parents planned on having him spend the night. At least we thought he was a friend. To my amazement and beyond my comprehension, he tried to sexually seduce me. You see this man stayed overnight in my bedroom. I had two double beds in my room and while I was asleep, I awoke and realized he was in my bed. I asked him what he was doing and he said, "I want to caress you." I said, "You better get out of my bed before I smash you." The man I am talking about was not only trusted by my parents and other members of my family, but trusted in his profession. His image led people to believe he was a man of God because he was an ordained priest. Later, a dear brother in Christ led me to the following Scriptures concerning this horrifying event, "Without natural affection, trucebreakers, false accusers, incontinent, fierce, despisers of those that are good, Traitors, heady, high-minded, lovers of pleasures more than lovers of God; having a form of godliness, but denying the power thereof: from such turn away" (2 Timothy 3:3-5).

I never told anyone about this violation in my life because I was too ashamed to talk about it. If only I had realized I should have sought God and sought a faithful and trusting individual to share my feelings of hurt, despair, and condemnation. I wish I had known that God is a God of restoration and love and He will completely heal and free you from any heaviness, guilt, or unresolved issues in your life. "He healeth the broken in heart, and bindeth up their wounds" (Psalm 147:3).

Looking back at my family life, I wonder what kept our family together. I knew God was in our lives, but why was He so merciful to my family? I realized my family's intercessory prayers to Jesus Christ were the glue that bonded us and kept us together. There were many who prayed, but my other grandmother set a powerful example. She had a heart for prayer and counted each blessing, each morsel of life, with thanksgiving to God. She had a hard and demanding life and experienced much suffering and brokenness, but God in turn used her powerfully to touch the lives of many, many people. She was so loving and caring to everyone, and you didn't have to qualify to be loved by her because she welcomed everybody. I used to sit and talk with her for hours, and sometimes she'd talk about her own experiences. I was totally engrossed in them. All in all, she reassured me with her loving ways and with her commitment, which was a reflection of the love and compassion of Jesus.

As time went on, an inner healing took place. I have found that it isn't until we cast all our cares on Jesus that we are completely healed. "Come unto me, all ye that labor and are heavy laden, and I will give you rest. Take my yoke upon you, and learn of me; for I am meek and lowly in heart: and ye shall find rest unto your souls. For my yoke is easy, and my burden is light" (Matthew 11:28-30).

As years passed, I grew closer to my parents and realized how much they meant to me, especially through my depression years later. They were instrumental in assisting me with my growth.

The growth I am talking about is my self-esteem. My dad used to say, "Oh, son, you can't attempt to work in that field, you don't know how to, and you don't have any experience with it." That was the whole point. I realized I couldn't and my dad's comments quickened me to push myself and prove to him and myself I could do anything I set my mind to do. My father indirectly gave me a "can do" attitude. The kinds of things I'm talking about related to either work, sports, or volunteering my services to an organization. After I would accomplish a goal, he'd always say, "Good job, son." Even when I did fail the first time, I had reassurance from God that I could complete what I had started. "I can do all things through Christ which strengtheneth me" (Philippians 4:13).

I grew up with one brother, who was two years older than I, and for the first fifteen years of my life he would never let me forget it. In my estimation, he was a bully. I could not figure out how two brothers could fight this way. We would go at it, and I would be the one who got the blame because my brother was the favorite of the family. After he would beat me up, then I'd run into the woods and hide. When I returned home, I would get into more trouble for running away. Of course my parents just didn't understand that my brother terrified me. Though I didn't like the treatment, I still loved my brother. To be able to overcome our differences was part of growing up. "And be ye kind one to another, tenderhearted, forgiving one another, even as God for Christ's sake hath forgiven you" (Ephesians 4:32).

As years progressed, I spent more time with my brother, mostly by helping him. We worked together wiring his family room at his new house. Our next project was rewiring his second house along with some grading work. The project took many hours, but I enjoyed being with him and his family. When we needed each other, we were there for one another. He supported me when I went through hard times. Whenever I'd call him on the phone, he'd always be available to listen and comfort me. "Let brotherly love continue" (Hebrew 13:1). God has a way of bringing the best out of people and drawing them closer together.

Chapter 2

Grammar School

I was taught the normal public kindergarten and grammar school curriculum, but in second grade my schooling took a turn. I was attending a local grammar school one mile from my house. During the parent-teacher conferences, my teacher discussed my progress with my mom and she concluded I was doing fine in class. However, despite her comments during the school year, which were positive, at the end of the year the teacher changed her opinion, She advised my mom that I had fallen behind, and it would be in my best interest to stay back a year. She also suggested that I go for a speech test, a hearing test, and a full battery of evaluations.

The testing included much more than was originally recommended. The person that performed the testing found a hearing disorder and arranged for me to have my ears flushed and cleaned. My parents were amazed at the buildup in my ear canal. I thought it was gross. Nevertheless I could hear so much better. Thank God for my parents following through.

I returned to school in the fall to attend second grade again. The events of the school year turned out the same as the previous year. My mom was told I was doing fine throughout the year and at the end was advised I needed to stay back again. My parents decided, thank God, that they weren't going to put me through the same routine. So, I was transferred to a private school for third grade. I absolutely loved my teacher at my new school. She was the greatest. As a matter of fact, she ended up being the best teacher I ever had, and I learned a lot in third grade. She treated me with love and respect. I, in turn, respected her and admired her, even at a very young age, because she was a sensitive and caring person.

I looked forward to school in third grade. This one year of love I received carried me through the next five years of torture I was about to experience in school. Little did I know what was in store for me in fourth grade. I went from loving school to hating it. I was transferred to a parochial school to be given further religious education. My parents didn't think I was getting enough religion at the time. I wondered who instilled that thought in their heads. They said that taking Sunday school classes after church wouldn't give me a sufficient education about God.

So I went from receiving love in school to receiving condemnation and fear. The teachers had a new method of teaching and discipline. They ruled in anger and force when you did something wrong. For example, I threw a snowball in the recess yard one wintry day, and I was taken to the office and told to hold out both hands, The teacher hit my hands with a ruler and made them sting. Sometimes the rulers would break from the force when she hit someone in the hand. I was treated with no more respect than a caged animal. Where was the respect that I was given in private school? How I longed to be back at the school I loved. Other times I would get slapped with the teacher's ring, which had an inlaid cross of Christ's crucifixion on it. Two of the teachers I had were sincere. The other four were beyond belief. From morning to afternoon I was locked up in a new world, a world of fear and disbelief. I learned quickly I needed to study just enough to pass for the year.

That went on year after year. I had no motivation any more, from fourth grade to the day I left in the eighth grade. In eighth grade I remember someone in front of me talking out of turn. When the teacher heard him, she came over to him and said, "You were talking, mister," and proceeded to literally beat him by slapping him and dragging him bodily out of the classroom. Wasn't this the institution of religious education where I was sent to learn about God? You would think that the physical abuse would be enough, but this boy also got suspended from school.

During the five years I attended parochial school, I used to look out the window, daydreaming about working on the farm across the street from my house, operating the tractors, plowing, disking, and preparing the seedbed and planting. I needed an escape from the fear and trials of hell on earth in the classroom. I didn't have a clue what was going on in my younger years, but I know now I should have shared these horrifying experiences with my parents.

At a young age I was being formed by God to be an overcomer, even though I wasn't aware of the molding in progress by Him. I would go to school in the morning on the bus, get off the bus at school and dream about being on the bus at the end of the school day. The harsh words and the physical abuse from the teachers brought a huge amount of fear into my life. The atmosphere at school upset me day after day. I had only two activities at school I enjoyed–lunch and recess.

Let me share one of the difficult lessons I had to learn. During the week, my class would have to walk to the affiliated church for church services, singing, and various religious lessons. On a particular day we were going to be instructed on confessing our sins. We finally arrived in church and were lined up, single file. The teacher turned to me in front of practically the whole school and said, "Practice your confession out loud." My confession went like this: "Bless me, Father, for I have sinned. It has been two weeks since my last confession and these are my sins. I have been disobedient to my parents, and I have fought with my brother." I finished and was standing in embarrassment and terror. The teacher then said to me, "Is that all?" I answered yes and thought about how small and upset I felt. I couldn't believe how heartless this teacher was. Actually I made up the confession just to have something to say, but I still felt totally stupid.

Another interesting teaching was when we sang. We had to sing so loud, and if we didn't, the teacher would say, "Louder, Louder." Why didn't she know you could damage your vocal cords if you sang too loud? Who were we actually singing to? God isn't deaf.

The truth concerning forgiveness of sins is found in the Word of God: "If we confess our sins, He is faithful and just to forgive us our sins, and to cleanse us from all unrighteousness" (1 John 1:9).

The scripture means exactly what is written. The Word directs us to confess our sins and says: "He is faithful and just to forgive us our sins."

I learned about true forgiveness of sins which can only come from God, not from a man-made format or agenda.

Chapter 3

Miracles at the Marina

When I was young, my family spent weekends on our cabin cruiser at the marina. On Fridays, my mom had to have everything ready for my father when he came home from the office. Our dog had to be taken to the vet, the food prepared and the clothes packed.

We all needed to be waiting at the front door. Once my dad got home, he greeted us and right away changed his clothes, loaded up the car and we were off to the boat–my mom, dad, brother and me. Boating was fun. My father was very well-versed in piloting the boat and charting the courses we were going to take. He was meticulous about having everything repaired and the engines in fine tune before we ventured out onto the ocean. I enjoyed running the boat from the fly bridge. It was an exciting experience. God has always been with us and protected us.

One early morning, while we were docked at the marina, I woke up and noticed an electrical fire in one of the receptacles. I yelled to my parents and quickly grabbed the fire extinguisher. They said, "No," and poured water on the electrical fire. They could have been electrocuted! Evidently, rain water had seeped into the receptacle to start the fire. With hundreds of gallons of fuel in the fuel tanks, the fire could have turned out to be a major disaster had it occurred in the middle of the night, when we were all sleeping. We were all thankful to God it didn't start until the morning.

Another blessing occurred when my parents and relatives were out on the ocean in the fog and couldn't see in front of them. Suddenly, my uncle yelled, "Hard port!" and my father swung the wheel hard to the left. As he did, the United States Coast Guard training ship, *The Eagle*, passed by them within feet and kept on going. Had they not made visual contact with the vessel, the ship would have cut their thirty-three foot craft in half without fazing the huge ship.

This near-collision was avoided because of the mighty and merciful hand of God. I can't imagine the repercussions had they collided. Many people could have been injured or perished in a matter of minutes. "With a strong hand, and with a stretched out arm: for his mercy endureth forever" (Psalms 136:12).

Where our boat was docked, there were two good sized swimming pools. One sunny day when I was about nine years old, I was swimming in one of the pools while the lifeguard was on the poolside talking with some other kids. After swimming for a while around the shallow end of the pool, I decided to venture out a bit into the deeper water.

I thought I was being careful about not going out too far, but before I knew it I was under water, and my feet couldn't touch bottom anymore. I struggled to reach the surface and saw the lifeguard watching me. I thought to myself, *Isn't she coming out to rescue me?* I continued to surface and sink to the bottom a few times. I was desperate and totally fearful that I was going to drown. Then I panicked and gave up all hope. I thought that there was nothing I could do, that I was going to die.

Finally, the lifeguard realized I wasn't fooling around and swam out to rescue me. By then I was chocking on water I had swallowed. I finally asked her, "Didn't you see me drowning?" She answered, "I thought you were kidding."

Needless to say, I was extremely upset, but thankful God was looking out for me.

"The Lord is my rock, and my deliverer; my God, my strength, in whom I will trust; my buckler, and the horn of my salvation, and my high tower" (Psalm 18:2).

Chapter 4

Physical Abuse

One weekend our family planned a Sunday dinner at my grand-parents' house. We were all looking forward to sharing some time together. I was ten years old at the time and anticipating a fun day with my cousins.

After Sunday services we came home, changed our clothes, and hurried to our dinner engagement. We greeted one another and sat down for dinner, which was a special time to share with one another. My grandmother had prepared a delicious dinner, which added to the festivities.

After dinner, my cousin and I decided to take a hike with the neighborhood kids. We didn't know at the time that they were the neighborhood troublemakers. All together there were about eight of us. So we started out for the woods for what I envisioned would be a great adventure. As soon as we entered the woods, the leader took off his belt. I was shocked. His belt was his weapon for the most part along with his foul mouth and disposition.

For the next forty-five minutes, I experienced hell, as he used his belt with no discretion. I felt the sting of the belt as he lashed out when we tried to escape. He assigned two other guards under him. We continued to try to escape from them, but when the guards got a notion we were planning something, they would advise the leader. He would put the whip into action and whip us again. He would scream as he whipped us as though we were a herd of wild animals. The hike through the woods turned out to be a frantic walk of fear. Finally, after almost an hour, it was over, and we could return home. The leader informed us that if we told our parents, he would whip us again. Consequently, we never told anyone.

This was truly an experience of terror and abuse. But I learned that anyone who has been abused in any way should not keep the pain locked up inside himself. Turn to Jesus and give Him all your pains, hurts and fears, for He is waiting to comfort you. "Blessed are they that mourn: for they shall be comforted" (Matthew 5:4). Jesus is our healer. "He healeth the broken in heart, and bindeth up their wounds" (Psalm 147:3). When we share the truth about our circumstances with the Lord, and with others, our openness in sharing allows us to be set free from our sufferings. It will loose us from the bondages and oppressions of guilt and fear, and it will enable us to be healed. "And ye shall know the truth, and the truth shall make you free" (John 8:32).

Chapter 5

Seasonal Farm Job

One day, my brother and I asked my father if we could work during the summer instead of spending the time boating. So my father decided to sell the boat and take up golfing.

During my summer vacation, I was available to work on a nearby vegetable farm. Across the street from our home, a farmer leased two five-acre parcels of land. The main farm property, consisting of forty-two acres, was located one mile from our house. I used to see the kids across the street working the fields, running big farm tractors and other machinery, and I couldn't wait for the opportunity to be part of the action.

I was very persistent once I was hired, continuing to ask my boss to teach me to operate the tractors. It finally paid off. I started out cultivating crops with a small tractor. Soon after, I was taught to run the bigger ones and learned to plow, disk harrow, fertilize, seed, spray herbicides and insecticides. I also hauled vegetable plants to various fields for planting.

I loved working on the farm so much I thought I was dreaming. I also enjoyed planting out in the fields with the other kids, but working in the greenhouse was more of a chore. I loved the work despite my boss's verbal abuse, especially when he'd call me names and get angry if I damaged or broke a part on the equipment.

One day, when I was just starting out on a cultivator, I clipped about a dozen cornstalks. I jumped off the tractor and replanted them, but they had no roots and soon were withered. My boss showed up shortly after to check up on me and see how I was doing. He noticed the dead corn plants and started yelling, "What did you do that for?" I started to say something and then he started in with the usual foul language. I just wanted to say I was sorry, but he never wanted to hear my response. I overlooked his anger and harsh words the best I could, because I loved the work.

The result of my overlooking his disposition was beneficial. My boss had many positive attributes and I admired him for being honest with me and for having confidence in me. He had more confidence in me than anyone else I knew. On a routine basis I would ask him, after working all day, if he was behind with any of the tractor work. His answer quite often was yes, so that allowed me to spend hours running the tractors through the night. Thank God my parents allowed me to work as much as I did.

Whenever I thought I could repair a machine, he'd say go ahead and never questioned my abilities. He also never expected me to pay for a broken part. I learned a valuable lesson from someone who would trust a kid to do a man's repair. I grew in confidence working with him.

My boss knew how to raise vegetables. Because he was efficient and because God is faithful, the harvest was always plentiful. He put his heart and soul into his work. The harvest was the most demanding time of the job, trying to make sure the thirty-one acres of vegetable crops were all brought in before the frost. I ended up working from early spring through the summer and into the fall season, pretty much every year for seventeen years.

During my younger years, when I had to contend with school, I just dreaded the thought of returning to school in the fall. Though I had many other jobs through- out the years, I always tried to find time to help out on the farm. I didn't know at the time of Jesus' parables of the sower.

I learned that the whole concept of sowing is an interesting and serious example of God's work, because in the parables of the sower Jesus refers to the seed as being the word of God. "Now the parable is this: The seed is the word of God. Those by the way side are they that hear; then cometh the devil, and taketh away the word out of their hearts, lest they should believe and be saved. They on the rock are they, which, when they hear, receive the word with joy; and these have no root, which for a while believe, and in time of temptation fall away. And that which fell among thorns are they, which, when they have heard, go forth, and are choked with cares and riches and pleasures of this life, and bring no fruit to perfection. But that on the good ground are they, which in an honest and good heart, having heard the word, keep it, and bring forth fruit with patience" (Luke 8:11-15).

We are commissioned to go forth and sow the seed of the word of God in the hearts of people. After we sow the seed, we are responsible to pray for the individuals to ensure that the seed will be watered and nurtured in conjunction with discipleship.

Chapter 6

Carelessness Leads to Injury

I had been working on our lawn and garden tractor for a number of hours, and I was anxious to complete the work. The job involved replacing the tractor's engine block, which involved more patience than I had. I was young at the time and couldn't wait to complete the job so I could use the tractor again. I was aligning the shroud on the flywheel because it was scraping, when I caught my left index finger and lacerated it.

I ran upstairs and showed my mom, who immediately washed out the cut and bandaged it. My mom had a friend over at the time, and they were chatting about their nursing experiences, so I felt like I was in good hands. My mom comforted me and asked me if I was feeling okay. I told her I felt faint, so she offered me something to eat.

She proceeded to cook up some spaghetti, which was one of my favorites. I thoroughly enjoyed my meal and began feeling better. After I finished eating, my mom's friend left and Mom and I headed for the emergency room.

It just so happened that my cousin, who was a surgeon at the hospital, was on duty when we arrived. He never was too pleasant when he treated me in the emergency room because he'd be angry with me about my carelessness. I guess that's just how he showed his concern for me. The advantage was that he meant well, and he was one of the best at his profession.

When he initially checked my mangled finger, he started to probe into the open wound with an instrument. Though I could hardly stand the pain, he asked me to move my finger as he continued to probe again and again. His diagnosis was that I had severed my muscle tendon, and he told me I would need to go into the operating room for surgery. He also told me I might have reduced use of the finger but we would hope for the best. My cousin advised me that his associate, on the hospital's medical staff, was going to handle my case because he was unable to perform the surgery due to a former commitment. What I anticipated to be a simple laceration requiring a few stitches turned out to be more than I had bargained for.

Early that evening, his associate finally came in, introduced himself and explained the whole procedure from start to finish. He said he would be operating that night. He continued to explain that I would be put under general anesthesia and would be spending the night in the hospital. His positive and gentle professional manner gave me a true sense of peace. He was concerned about my comfort, safety, and the success of the operation. He also made it perfectly clear that he was going to be up front and truthful with me.

I was prepped for the surgery and a nurse inserted an intravenous into my right arm. Shortly after that, I was given a muscle relaxant to help me calm down. It was the first time I had ever needed an operation. As I was being brought into the operating room, I got a little apprehensive about everything happening to me. The anesthesiologist connected me to the monitors and other equipment and started asking me questions. He asked if I had eaten any dinner, and when I told him I had eaten spaghetti, he answered with, "That's the worst meal you could have eaten." I was curious and asked him why. Then he said, "If you were to vomit, it could be dangerous because of the danger of choking." At least by now I was more tranquil because of the sedatives they gave me. So, I said okay to the next instruction to count to ten. I think I got to three and was out cold.

I woke up in the recovery room, hours later, asking the nurse to hold my hand. I remember asking her because I was scared as the anesthesia was wearing off. She was very reassuring, even though I felt embarrassed. She later told me not to be concerned about it, that I did just fine. Shortly after that, I was taken to my room. My mom and dad came in to see me and gave me a hug and kiss and reassured me with their love. The nurse came in and administered a medication to help me relax, and soon I was asleep. In the morning my doctor came by to check on my progress. He advised me that the operation went well and asked how I felt. I told him I was doing okay and appreciated his support. He said he was releasing me from the hospital in the afternoon and that he'd like to see me in his office the following week.

When I made my visit to his office, I found out I was able to move my finger. As time went on, I regained full movement. I was especially concerned about my injury because I wrote with my left hand, the one I injured. God is so great and faithful and I thank Jesus for bringing me through this time of need. "For I will restore health unto thee, and I will heal thee of thy wounds, saith the Lord" (Jeremiah 30:17).

Chapter 7

High School Abuse

My experiences of physical and emotional abuse in high school were horrendous.

Parochial school started out like being in a pressure cooker. Most of my classes were conducted by trained religious educators. I thought their purpose in the religious order was to serve God by educating students and by caring for others, but found out their main attention was devoted to serving and feeding their own egos. They had a violent method of educating students. In a French class, when I and the whole class started laughing, the teacher turned to me and called my name. I answered, "Yes," and he told me in front of the whole class that I laughed like a horse. He told me to go to the principal's office. Embarrassed and upset, I left the classroom.

Waiting at the principal's office, I felt like a prisoner. I ended up having to attend detention after school and faced possible suspension. I thought to myself that I was dreaming. I had already witnessed five years of repeated unethical discipline and now found myself on a roller-coaster ride of abusive treatment. Again I was right back in the same type of system with the teachers and administration exercising discipline only through bondage, fear, and violence. I began to wonder if I was really in a school based on religious education. What happened to the Christ-like mercy, forgiveness, love, and grace that is written about throughout the Bible? I was so deceived to think I needed to attend school here because my brother went here. I had already been subjected to fear, terror, and condemnation from my past schooling experiences, even though I tried to make the best of it.

A few days later while I was in another class, I spoke out of turn. The teacher walked over to me and said, "Were you talking?" As he asked me the question, he punched me in the chest and I started to cry. Actually, I believed I shouldn't have talked out of turn, but was this type of discipline really necessary? I was being schooled in an institution of hell. I couldn't believe my teacher or the pain he induced in my chest. I was then told to report to the office and this time got to sit down and face the principal. He stared at me and said, "You have a problem, mister!" I responded by saying, "I do?" He said, "You have a problem!" and proceeded to put me on detention again.

I knew at this point I just had to inform my parents of every horrendous detail regarding my difficulty with handling the abuses at school. Just for the record, the abusive chest- punching teacher struck other students other than me on a routine basis. Another day a teacher disciplined a student near me by physically dragging him out of the classroom by his hair, after violently striking him in other parts of his body. I thought, what are these teachers trying to prove by abusing the students this way? I couldn't wait for the opportunity to leave this deceptive form of correction and schooling. I was fearful and apprehensive of my next encounter with teachers who totally disregarded a student's well-being and human rights. "For God hath not given us the spirit of fear; but of power, and of love, and of a sound mind" (2 Timothy 1:7).

I explored the possibility of attending another school, with my parent's help, because when I told them I hated this school, they were very supportive of the change and wanted the best for me. A local trade school had an opening for a freshman. I could hardly wait for the opportunity to leave the ungodly mess I was in. After being treated like a wild animal, I was soon to be treated with respect. The teachers at my new school were real people, and for the first time since third grade I was accepted. I could now shed my fear and terror, and the shackles of hell were released.

God was and is so very faithful.

Chapter 8

Trade School Blessings
and Miracles

After transferring from parochial school to trade school, my desire was to learn about the electrical trade. At the time, the electrical shop was filled to capacity, so I was asked to choose between the automotive, machine, drafting, or carpentry shops. I was also advised that the electrical shop would probably have a slot open in my sophomore year. I selected the carpentry shop. I spent two weeks there and rotated the next two weeks in related academic studies. I might add that at my previous school, I was in the very bottom freshmen grade level. At trade school, I was placed in the highest grade level, so I was off to a better start.

I enjoyed trade school and respected all the instructors and teachers. Everyone had a unique regard for the students, including the entire administrative staff, nurse, janitorial crew, kitchen staff, librarian, and even the substitutes. They genuinely cared about you. At times I thought I was dreaming. It was time to move on and concentrate on learning and push aside all the negativity I experienced in the schools I attended in the past. "Remember ye not the former things, neither consider the things of old" (Isaiah 43:18).

I didn't realize this at the time, but God spoke to me years later and told me: "You are a child of God, and everything you went through I went through with you." I knew there had to be a reason, a purpose, for why I was able to get through so many trials. The darkness of my earlier school days and the fear of the unknown had been transformed into a season of daily brightness and peace.

As time went on, I especially enjoyed the hours I spent in the carpentry shop. We built various wood projects, and it was fun as I learned to work with my hands.

One day my shop instructor told me about his plans to build a single-family home during the summer months. He told me that he was planning to hire a helper and asked me if I'd be interested in helping him with the framing portion of the project. I immediately answered him without a split second of hesitation, yelling out a big yes. He advised me that he'd keep me informed of the project and my starting date. I didn't realize this until years later, but God had given me favor with my teacher.

Out of four classes, including the freshman, sophomore, junior, and senior students, my instructor selected me to assist him with the summer project. To God, I sincerely give the thanksgiving and the glory! It was an oversight on my part, at the time, not to recognize how much God was really doing for me. Now I know the truth of: "The Lord bless thee, and keep thee: The Lord make his face shine upon thee, and be gracious unto thee: The Lord lift up his countenance upon thee, and give thee peace" (Numbers 6:24-26). At the time I simply felt excited to think that I was actually going to work with my instructor on a summer construction project.

As summer approached I couldn't wait for what was in store for me. I knew my farm job would be waiting for me, but now I had a new opportunity and a new challenge. Finally I received a call to report to work. Being his student through the year, I knew he was a resourceful teacher, leading me and guiding me through each task and each technique at hand. It was now my opportunity to make use of some of the skills I was developing.

This was my first experience with actually building a house. I was the youngest worker on the job, and all the workers were very helpful. They assisted me and encouraged me whenever I had a need. We all worked very hard. I loved the challenge and looked forward to participating with the project each day. Some days I just cleaned the job site, stacked lumber, or back-nailed, with some jobs being more interesting than others. No matter what job I was assigned to, I was still given the same respect and knew I was a part of the team effort.

Construction Miracle

One day, I was working with the men setting floor joists in place. Suddenly a man began screaming and shaking, and bouncing up and down on the timbers. Thinking he was experiencing a seizure, I grabbed him to ensure he wouldn't fall into the basement. I didn't know at the time he was being electrocuted. Both of us now were getting electrocuted.

Right away, one of the workers yelled to me to pull the plug. Actually, he was the one that should have pulled the plug. The only way I was able to break away from the flow of the electrical current was from the hand of God. I finally let go and ran for the plug. As soon as I grabbed the plug to pull it out, I received another electric shock. I was hesitant because I didn't want the man to get any further injuries than he had already sustained from the electricity, but I was the closest person to the service panel. As soon as I pulled the plug, he immediately fell into the basement. He was in agonizing pain. We rushed over to remove his tool belt and make him as comfortable as possible. Meanwhile a worker ran next door and called an ambulance.

Soon, the ambulance arrived and took the man to the emergency room. He remained conscious through the whole ordeal, despite the severe pain. The electricity affected the muscles in his body, and he remained in the hospital for months. We found out the electrical shock was caused by an incorrectly wired power tool. He was finally released from the hospital and, to the best of my knowledge, is fully recovered.

God's hand saved the workman miraculously from disability and death. "By stretching forth thine hand to heal; and that signs and wonders may be done by the name of thy holy child Jesus" (Acts 4:30).

As time progressed, we continued to work building the house with one less man, whom we all missed very much. It took a while to learn to focus on the job and not be continually thinking and talking about our coworker. When we had set all the rafters in place and sheathed the roof with plywood, my job came to an end. I worked on the project for two months and was so blessed to have been given this opportunity. I finished the summer by working on the farm, which I enjoyed also.

In my sophomore year at trade school, I was accepted into the electrical shop. I had discussed my desire with my carpentry instructor, and he suggested I follow my desire to learn the electrical trade. I met my new shop instructor during orientation. I started my first week in the electrical shop and learned that this was the year when regular training commenced. As a freshman you learned the basics of the trades and toured each trade to assist you with your selection of the one you desired. I found out I hadn't missed too much from not being in the electrical shop until then.

The first couple of weeks we got acquainted with the basic tools of the trade and were required to purchase our own set of tools. That was exciting. Next, we learned about the various wiring methods and practiced them in the small studded room built inside the electrical shop. I got along with the instructor quite well, mainly because I was so interested in learning about the electrical trade and was totally engrossed in his instructions. My instructor continued to be a blessing.

As I got more acquainted with the electrical shop, I learned we'd be actually working on a residential wiring job. I almost fell off my chair I was so excited. Each day, when I was in my academic classes, I'd count the days until I'd be back in shop. Finally, we were at a point in the electrical shop to load up the shop bus and head out to the job site. The anticipation was overwhelming, I wondered what task I'd be assigned to when we reached the job site.

When we arrived at the job site, which was a lovely home in the country, the instructor got everyone started on their respective tasks. He then turned to me and said, "Let's go into the cellar." I wondered what I was going to work on in the cellar. The main electrical service, which consisted of two one-hundred-ampere circuit breaker panels, were installed in the cellar. My instructor turned to me and said, "Your job will be to bring the circuit cables into the panels and connect them to the circuit breakers. After I show you the procedures you'll be all set." I learned the methods and the procedures one at a time and felt comfortable with doing the work.

I didn't realize at the time I was again being given God's favor. There were experienced upper classmen on the job site, but I was chosen. There were dangers involved with the task because the electrical panels were energized; nevertheless I continued doing the work. A few moments later, the instructor's son, who was a junior at the time, came over to talk to me. I had favor with him also. He took me under his wing and helped me a great deal. To have an upper-class student as a buddy was a definite plus. As we were talking, one of the bare ground wires managed to land in the energized panel. The wire caused a short circuit, which flashed and slightly melted a spot on the panel buss bar. My instructor ran over to me and told me to please be careful and turned to his son and told him not to bother me.

I just knew this was it. After making this mistake, I doubted that I would be allowed to complete the wiring of the panels. The procedure involved installing the cables into the panel, connecting the ground and neutral wire to their respective ground bars, connecting the power conductors to the appropriate circuit breakers, labeling the panel to identify the circuits and completing the project by energizing the circuits and testing each one. I didn't think I was going to possibly complete the project, especially after making a major mistake. I was resigned to the fact that I'd be given a different task or be told to wait in the bus until it was time for everyone to leave the job site. Everything happened so quickly, as do many accidents that occur from negligence. My instructor turned to me and said, "Let's take a look at the damage in the panel," and then proceeded to scrape the bus bar to clean it. The next thing my instructor said to me was to be extra careful and concentrate on my work.

I was completely caught off guard. How could a teacher be so forgiving, when I had made such a major mistake? It was hard for me to comprehend, but it was really happening. I was so blessed. Thank the Lord!

I continued working on the panel wiring for the rest of the day and then it was time to load up and return to school. On the way back I thought about what had taken place during the day and the new sense of accomplishment I felt.

Because of my previous first-aid training, which was a prerequisite to joining the National Ski Patrol, I asked my electrical shop instructor if I could teach a class at school on artificial resuscitation, for all those students who were enrolled in the electrical program. He said, "Sure," and gave me special permission to be excused from any academic classes for the periods scheduled during the first-aid lessons.

I taught four grade levels and for the most part, despite a few wisecracks, everything went according to plan. I gave lessons on the steps to perform artificial resuscitation and told the class they would be given a practical and a written test, which would count toward their grade. I used a mannequin to demonstrate the procedures and everyone in the four classes did a great job. I appreciated the confidence my teacher had in me, to allow me to teach.

Years after I graduated, my shop instructor in my sophomore year assisted and tutored me to prepare for my state electrical license exams. He also continued to help me whenever I asked for assistance many years later. He was a huge support in my life.

In my junior year, I had a new instructor, and he was an excellent teacher also. He was a man of very few words, but what he did say was to the point. He always went to bat for us. He fought the system to enable the electrical students to take on a machine shop wiring project. The job required the installation of a four-hundred-ampere main service, load centers, buss ways, lighting, receptacles, heating, and all the machine wiring. In the past, we were only allowed to be involved in residential projects. I was enthusiastic about being part of a major project.

Our instructor was very thorough and demanding. He said we were there to learn, and he would cover all the material necessary to prepare and equip us. I enjoyed the various experiments, which involved wiring and troubleshooting. I also enjoyed the challenges of class.

One day a student was charging a heavy-duty battery. He evidently was sweating and was handling two of the DC leads from a rectifier with his bare hands and there was no insulation on them. The student was screaming and shaking. He couldn't let go. I knew this was serious. I was standing close to him but couldn't get at the power cord or the shut-off switch on the rectifier. I quickly got into position to launch myself into him to break the connection. As I did he immediately fell to the floor and was saved from the dangerous current. He was unhurt but upset. Our shop instructor stood there through the whole episode and finally said, "See what happens when you're not careful?"

I finally reached over and found the switch to turn the rectifier off. I thank God for His protection over us. "The Lord is my strength and my shield; my heart trusted in him, and I am helped: therefore my heart greatly rejoiceth; and with my song will I praise Him" (Psalm 28:7).

Chapter 9

Miracles on the Highway

One weekend, my family decided to visit my relatives overnight. So the four of us packed up and headed out, looking forward to an enjoyable time.

My cousin invited me, together with her friends, to attend a ski club movie at the local high school. My cousin's girl friend picked us up at her house, and we anticipated a fun evening.

I noticed right away that the driver was very careless as she sped down the secondary roads. I asked her to slow down but she told me, "It's all right." As she continued to drive at a high rate of speed, she told us that she didn't want to get to the movie late. We were traveling through country roads at more than sixty miles per hour and she was continuing to accelerate. We yelled at her to slow down but she wouldn't listen to anyone. All of a sudden, she hit a bump in the road and the car swerved. Next, she panicked and instead of applying the brakes she continued to speed even more. I looked at the speedometer and yelled, "You are going to kill us!"

We were all yelling at her to slow down, all four passengers, but she had panicked when we hit the bump and pressed the accelerator to the floor instead of using the brakes. When I looked at the speedometer once more from the back seat, it read between seventy and seventy-five miles per hour, I thought that it was all over, that we were all going to die.

Then came the terrible crash, right into the side of the roadway, which was a solid rock ledge. It was like hitting a thick wall of concrete. Everyone at this point was unconscious. We rolled completely over once and landed back on the tires with a loud crash.

All four occupants of the vehicle regained consciousness. I asked everyone if they had any injuries and how they felt. Even though we were all in shock, which could have led to complications, none of us had hardly a scratch. Each of us was able to get out of the vehicle, through the four car doors, despite the fact that the car was totally demolished.

Though the car was wrecked beyond belief, there was no smell of any gasoline leaks nor any smoke or fire either. After the accident, we all were taken to the emergency room and checked out and soon released. We all knew it was a miracle, guided by the hand of Jesus Christ, to have survived such a violent collision. Everyone realized we were so blessed by being able to walk away from the accident. "Yea, though I walk through the valley of the shadow of death, I will fear no evil: for thou art with me: thy rod and thy staff they comfort me" (Psalm 23:4).

On another occasion while driving on an interstate highway one frigid evening, I lost control of my sports car. The main portion of the highway was not icy, but while driving over a bridge my car started to spin uncontrollably. Suddenly I heard God speak to me: "Just hold the steering wheel". As I did the car spun 360 degrees three times and ended up on an exit ramp, undamaged. I was scared because there was traffic at a distance behind me and I thought I was going to crash.

Chapter 10

Depression

While attending a high school dance one Saturday evening, I thought maybe I would meet someone special. Well, I did meet someone and she turned out not to be the special young lady I had envisioned she would be. I was then sixteen years old and in my junior year in high school. I was introduced to the girl through another friend. We danced and had fun throughout the evening together, with our other friends. Then we decided to get together again at the end of the dance and I told her I'd be calling during the following week.

I did call her and we started dating–going to the movies, and parties, and just having fun together. After a period of time, we began to get more serious and she decided it was time. She would drop a few hints and make some advances, but I ignored the fact that she had sex on her mind. I could have just said no and left it at that, but I thought I loved her and enjoyed being with her. What did I know at sixteen? This experience took place in the early seventies. We continued to date and we continued to become more emotionally involved with each other. I couldn't stand to be away from her. All I thought about was her. She would say that we needed to be careful, and I would say okay, being a bit naive at the time. I knew her desires and I ignored them. She, on the other hand, was determined and we started fighting quite often. I was brought up believing sex wasn't an option in my life until I married. In the Scripture, 1 Corinthians 6:18, it reads, "Flee fornication. Every sin that a man doeth is outside the body; but he that committeth fornication sinneth against his own body."

When I wouldn't commit or respond to her sexual desires, she would get back at me by being critical and hurtful through verbal abuse. The smart and wise thing for me to have done would have been to tell her our relationship was over. But I cared for her and was emotionally involved with her. As each week went by, I received more and more demeaning comments from her and in turn I became more and more depressed. I lost interest in some areas of my life. My girlfriend continued to hammer away at me with her negative abusive routine.

My dad noticed a change in me. He was concerned that I wasn't smiling too much and I acted so somber. Finally my dad asked me if I'd like to talk to someone who was coming over for dinner. A psychiatrist from a foreign culture, who was a friend of the family, would be able to talk to me after dinner. I told my dad I'd be happy to share my feelings with the doctor. I enjoyed dinner with my parents and our company, and after dinner the doctor and I sat in my room and had a discussion. He asked me how I was doing. I told him I was brought up not to have sex before marriage because I was taught in the Catholic religion that premarital sex is a sin.

Then I started to spill my guts. I told him about my girlfriend. I told him the whole story, after we talked for a while and I had gained trust in him. This wasn't the first time I'd met this doctor either, so it wasn't too difficult to share my thoughts. He was studying me as I was expressing myself to him. I told him my Christian beliefs and said I was upset with my girlfriend, who didn't understand, that she just knew what she wanted and didn't care about my feelings. I also told him that I felt I was taking a beating emotionally.

He then asked me if I was depressed. My answer was yes. He said: "Have you wanted to commit suicide?" I answered yes, but that I didn't kill myself because of the love I had for my parents. I answered these questions in tears. I just couldn't stop crying. He asked me how I would have committed suicide? I said with one of the guns in my bedroom closet. I then pointed to the closet. I owned a spear gun, a 20-gauge shotgun, a 22-caliber rifle, and a pellet rifle. He told me to stay put for a minute and called to my parents upstairs.

My parents came downstairs and the doctor told them the situation regarding my depression. He asked them to remove the weapons from my closet and to lock them up in a safe place. Our conversation continued, and I was unaware he was going to use me as a specimen for his own research. Maybe it was normal to him what he proposed and planned for my treatment. But I realize now that I should have sought a second opinion from a Christian counselor. He explained to me I would be taking Thorazine, a tranquilizer, in high dosages. Also, I would be taking a mood stimulant called Elavil and other medications as needed. The medications were going to sedate me, actually beyond belief.

In the next thirty days I gained sixty pounds. Mostly, I would sleep, wake up, and have just about enough energy to eat and go back to sleep. The medications increased my appetite enormously together with my constant need to sleep. Without any exercise, I blew up like a balloon. The side effects caused my mouth to be as dry as rope. I was de-personalized because I lost my identity. Also, my hands and legs didn't feel like they were part of me. I could hardly read. Even though I had to get prescription glasses, I had no energy to read, write, or watch television. My hands would shake uncontrollably. My muscles were stiff and my legs were so uncomfortable. I had uneasy nervous feelings throughout my entire body. The sensations were hard to describe. I was in so much pain that at times I moaned and tossed and turned in bed for what seemed like hours. I felt like screaming at times but didn't have the energy to do so. I was often faint and could only walk a short distance in my house. Other horrible side effects, which I started experiencing later on in my therapy, were nightmares and massive migraines, and they were very hard to control.

The doctor visited me each day and interpreted my dreams and told me I was coming along. I remember a dream I had. There were sharks circling in clear blue water and someone directing them. I believe the director in the dream was Jesus and the blueness was heavenly character. The sharks were the enemy and though they were circling, they were not able to pursue their prey, which was me.

God's heavenly character prevented me from committing suicide. I understood God's character to be one of love. The love I had for my parents prevented me from pulling the trigger. God instilled that love in me through the relationship I had with my parents. Had I not been hurt so many times and received that comfort from my parents, I don't even want to speculate about what could have happened to me during my severe depression.

My doctor told me a different interpretation, which didn't make any sense. He also told my parents to keep God out of my therapy. The doctor was operating in the flesh and he cared nothing about God. It disturbed me that he was trying to treat my depression without God, but I was so heavily medicated I couldn't even reason with him. He told me if he gave a horse the amount of drugs I was given, the animal would die. What was that supposed to mean, other than he was out of his mind and I was being compared with an animal?

According to my doctor, there were two areas of my life I had to ignore: one was God and the other was my girlfriend. The girl I understood fully, but when it came to God, my doctor trying to alienate me from my faith and my moral beliefs, I thought he was the one who should have been in therapy. Had I gone to the right counselor or doctor, I doubt I would have been asked to give up on God and I don't think I would have been processed like an animal and given such large doses of medications. In the depths of my soul, I knew I was never going to give up on Him, What I really needed was someone to talk to and pray with. As soon as I called my girlfriend and told her I wouldn't be seeing her any longer, I felt better. I didn't have to fight that battle any longer.

I wasn't able to work at my part-time job either, which upset me. I also heard that one of my close relatives spread an untruth about me, when she told people I was recovering from illicit uncontrolled drugs. Sometimes, families know just what it takes to enlarge the wound and pour salt on it. I wondered whatever gave her that indication.

Through many difficult times in my life, I always knew my parents, grandmother, and other family members were interceding in prayer to the Lord Jesus for me. My grandmother made me so happy when she came to visit me, especially when I was in need. She stayed at our house for weeks when I was sick, and I was so blessed. I loved talking to her and my mom. They helped me through the most difficult time in my life. My grandmother would say to me: "Every day, in every way, you're getting better and better." She'd always say, "I'm praying for you." Her sincere encouragement and love meant a lot to me.

During my therapy sessions, my doctor fed me with sin. He would tell me that it was perfectly natural to experience sexual relations while I was single. He said there was nothing wrong with it, and that I needed to disregard what I was taught in religious education.

At this point I was confused. What happened to the God I was serving? Although I wasn't using illegal drugs and wasn't indulging in alcohol, I was still in great danger. My spirit man was dying. My soul was being corrupted with the introduction of sexual sin suggestions, which was a disaster. At the time, I was so sedated I almost felt unconscious. I knew people were around me but most of the time I didn't have a clue as to what was happening to me. This was because of poor choices in my therapy. My doctor loved to medicate heavily with controlled drugs. The only problem was that he was the one controlling the doses. The doctor had no more faith than an animal.

I didn't realize it at the time, but I was being torn away from my Christian beliefs and from my concerns, needs, and desires to obey God. While I was medicated, I lost touch with God and reality. I got too involved with secular procedures and prescription drugs. I was turning to my doctor and thought he had all the answers, when actually he had none of the true answers I was looking for. My most vital need at the time of my depression was to be fed with spiritual food. I know now that "Man shall not live by bread alone, but by every word that proceedeth out of the mouth of God" (Matthew 4:4). A daily diet of manna from heaven was what

I really needed. I had faith because God had imparted faith into my life. He allowed me to stand up for Him and persevere.

After being sedated for over a month, my dad consulted with another doctor. They agreed the medication needed to be cut back. My dad asked me to visit another doctor. At this point, I didn't know what to think but agreed to the visit. I wondered what the doctor was going to say about my past therapy.

During my first visit to the next doctor, he couldn't figure out why I had been given so much medication. He immediately lowered my doses and said that I'd be fine. After all the torture I went through, this doctor couldn't give me a reason for the outrageously heavy doses. I told him I was having extreme nightmares, and his response was that I'd be all right. I asked him if there was something he could give me for my migraines, and he agreed to prescribe a new medication for me. That was just what I needed, another medication. I told him about my thought processes, and that I had unclear, impure, and sometimes confusing thoughts. He asked me, "Why do you have them?" and said that I shouldn't be having thoughts like that.

Then we got into the sexuality issue. The doctor told me, "Sex is fine, and it doesn't matter who you have sex with, male or female, everything goes," which is contrary to the Word. "For this cause God gave them up unto vile affections: for even their women did change the natural use into that which is against nature: And likewise also the men, leaving the natural use of women, burned in their lust one toward another; men with men working that which is unseemly, and receiving in themselves that recompence of their error which was meet" (Romans 1:26-27). I told him that I had a girlfriend prior to my depression, and we could end the conversation regarding sexual relations. I had heard enough from the other doctor who said the same thing.

"For we wrestle not against flesh and blood, but against principalities, against powers, against the rulers of the darkness of this world, against spiritual wickedness in high places" (Ephesians 6:12). I learned that when you don't follow the guidelines set up by Jesus Christ, but push Him out of your life, that Satan will then come into the situation. "The thief cometh not, but for to steal, and to kill, and to destroy: I am come that they might have life, and that they might have it more abundantly" (John10:10).

Years went by. I couldn't come to an understanding of what actually took place during the months of torture I endured. The suffering took place because I obeyed the Lord. God directed me to the answer in His word: "Then said Jesus unto his disciples, If any man will come after me, let him deny himself, and take up his cross, and follow me" (Matthew 16:24).

Denying oneself for Christ is more than we could ever bargain for. It is the price we need to pay to be used by God. Though the doctors pushed God out of my life for a season, God turned the whole situation around by allowing me to stand for what I believed. "And we know that all things work together for good to them that love God, to them who are the called according to his purpose" (Romans 8:28).

At times in our lives we need to turn to God. We also need to confide in a Christian counselor to help us, nurture us, direct us in Scripture, pray with us, and support us through any difficulties that we may encounter. Christian principles found in the Word of God and set into motion by a Christian professional could make one of the biggest positive differences in your life.

Chapter 11

Construction Job

Just before graduation from trade school in 1971, I asked a neighbor for a job working for him on construction. He had need–a laborer and truck driver on a large sewer line installation project in town–and I certainly needed some extra hard work to shed my excess weight. After talking with him briefly, he agreed to hire me and gave me a start date.

I ended up starting to work for him shortly after graduation. I was thrilled at the opportunity. He owned heavy, earth-moving equipment, which always interested me. The first day on the job, he sent me out to gather supplies for the project. Meanwhile his crews were moving the equipment to the job site and making final preparations for the commencement of the project. Because of the depth of the sewer flow line, which was engineered at twenty feet below the road surface, there were many issues to address.

An opening in the existing manhole was required and needed to be jack hammered. Trench safety boxes needed to be set in place to support the sidewalls of the excavation to prevent them from caving in. The utility companies were called to support the poles along the trench, and the street needed to be detoured. I didn't know what I was in for, being a kid right out of high school. While I was at the shop loading up a truck, the men from the job arrived with a tractor-trailer. I walked over and asked them how everything was going on the job, and they told me the road had collapsed and completely filled the first section of the trench box. They came with the truck and trailer to move the crane on site. So much of the road had collapsed that the excavator didn't have enough boom reach to reach the excavation. Evidently the road had collapsed because of the high water table. Thank God, no one was in the trench at the time. I finally arrived on site and was amazed at what was taking place. Almost two- thirds of the road had collapsed. As time progressed, the trench boxes were set in place, and we were ready to roll. In the existing manhole, the laser was set for grade and the opening in it was completed, the excavated trench was bedded with crushed stone, and we were ready to set the first length of clay pipe.

It was a slow process because the clay was so brittle that at times it would get broken while we were trying to set it. The other hindrance to the safety and productivity of the project was the steady flow of subsurface water pouring into the trench. Although we had pumps operating, we still had problems with the road undermining and caving in. The inspector on site was constantly monitoring the sidewalls of the excavation.

Other than the owners, two sons, and one regular employee, the workers on site didn't like to see me working hard and doing my job. As a matter of fact, one guy picked a fight with me and grabbed me by my raincoat the first day. Later in the day, I told the boss about it and he said, "One of you will just have to go." I knew what that meant, and I wasn't going to quit that easy. I learned to do my job, and the harder I worked the better I felt.

At times some of the guys would team up together to try to run me off the job but I elected to ignore them. We bedded the trench with crushed stone, then set the pipe and covered it with layers of sand, which had to be compacted. Sometimes when I worked in the trench, the operator of the loader would dump the full bucket of stone or sand in one place, which meant three yards of material for me to shovel. Sometimes the excavator operator would level it out, but if he had already moved ahead he couldn't reach it, so I had to shovel the extra material. Actually I didn't even care how much I had to shovel because I knew I was getting into shape.

One day, when I was about to go down into a manhole to remove a laser, the man who didn't like me too much walked over to me and said, "You know, I wouldn't think anything about killing you." I thought to myself, *I'd better not go into the manhole.* He said, "When no one is in the loader, you get in it and run it and when the dozer operator is standing right there, you get in and run it. What are you trying to do, take our jobs away?" I said, "You're right. When no one is running the equipment, I do it, because I'm here to do my job and get the job done." I then said to him that I'd see him later and started walking down the street until he was gone.

After a while we all learned to work together. The job went slowly due to the depth of the cut, the high water table, and the ledge we encountered, which required blasting.

The summer job had its trials, but I felt so blessed. I learned to operate trucks and heavy equipment, use lasers for setting grades, and in the first six weeks of working I lost the sixty pounds I had gained when I was sick.

I felt so much better once I lost the weight. I regained confidence in myself that I could continue to persevere when the going got rough. "Now unto him that is able to do exceeding abundantly above all that we ask or think, according to the power that worketh in us" (Ephesians 3:20).

Chapter 12

Beautifying the Yard

My parents had left this particular Friday afternoon and wouldn't be back until Saturday afternoon sometime. I had planned the tree removal to beautify the yard. Also when you drove down the driveway, the trees obstructed your view of the oncoming traffic, which was quite dangerous.

I had already lined up the equipment I needed and had gotten permission to dump any excess materials directly across the street from our house. I got up Saturday morning early, already planning to remove about twelve trees on our property along the roadside.

I borrowed a three-yard Caterpillar loader and a Mack truck with a cable winch. The trees were about twenty-five feet high. I used the winch cable on some of them to pull them over. On the larger ones I used the winch to direct their fall and then my friend and I would cut them up with a chain saw. Praise God for my prior summer job experience! The owner was very generous to let me use any piece of equipment I needed.

So I dug out the huge stumps with the loader and dumped them across the street. I also cut down and removed three large pine trees. The job was going just fine. All the trees were falling where we had planned. One concern I had was about a nearby primary power line. I knew the dangers involved and was extra cautious working around it. I was having a great time cutting and removing the stumps and brush, and grading the area.

Suddenly a car pulled up. It was my parents, who couldn't get in the driveway because the trees were blocking it. The driveway looked like a bomb had hit it because everything was so torn up.

I quickly pushed the trees out of the way and moved the truck so my parents could drive in. My dad and mom were upset and said, "What are you doing?" I said that I was cleaning up the yard so it will be safer when we drove down to the road and needed to have a better view of the oncoming traffic. Their answer was: "You didn't ask us." Even though my dad wasn't too keen about my particular work-related intentions, he usually wouldn't say no, but this time was different. I told my parents it was a surprise, but it turned out to be more of a shock to them than a surprise.

I knew if I said to them that I wanted to cut down twelve twenty-five-foot-high trees next to the road, and that a friend was going to help me, and that I was going to borrow a Caterpillar loader and a Mack truck with a heavy duty winch, and that my chain saw was serviced and sharpened, and that I had permission to dump the boulders, stumps, and other spoils across the street, and that I knew about the power-line dangers, and that I'd be careful working around the traffic, and that the work would enhance their property and it would be safer for us to see the oncoming cars, I knew the answer this time would have been positively *no*, period.

My parents drove on up to the house. My friend and I continued to complete the project, and everything would soon be done. The next day I finished grading and raking, seeded the ground and put mulch over the area. I made sure to return the equipment before Monday morning.

My dad and mom said to me, "Son it does look better." That's all I needed to make my job complete in my heart. I was now pleased because my parents recognized the result of the job.

The project turned out as I anticipated because God's hand led me through. He guided me in ways of dealing with my parents, which strengthened my relationship with them.

This was one of the many experiences in my life that were teaching experiences. I proceeded with my dreams with God's guidance, along with my mother's positive attitude, knowing my father would be positive once he realized what I was doing was possible and also practical. Growing up, I was always proving myself to my dad and to myself about what looked impossible to accomplish, but God was showing me: "With men this is impossible; but with God all things are possible" (Matthew 19:26).

I also learned at a very young age to always give God the glory by thanking Him for each and every blessing in my life. "Giving thanks always for all things unto God and the Father in the name of our Lord Jesus Christ" (Ephesians 5:20).

Chapter 13

Drinking and Driving

In my senior year in high school, though I was getting older, I was not necessarily becoming wiser. On Friday evenings my friends and I would drive just over the New York state line to purchase beer and other assorted liquors. I thought it was now time to party. I would drink and drive, with my friends in the car on the highway with the rock and roll music on full blast. It was just plain stupid, immature, and selfish of me to take chances jeopardizing so many people's lives. I was very fortunate that I didn't get into any accidents.

The realization of possibly killing, mutilating, or crippling someone is a reality I will never forget. Years later, when I began to grow up and realize my drinking and driving episodes could have turned into a disaster of death, I repented to Jesus Christ and asked for forgiveness of my sins. I knew I needed to appreciate life more and respect the lives of others to a deeper degree. "If we confess our sins, He is faithful and just to forgive us our sins, and to cleanse us from all unrighteousness." (1John 1:9).

As years passed, I learned to be more and more responsible. I decided I would go to work for an ambulance service. One of the prerequisites for working on the ambulance crew was emergency medical technician certification. The training course was being held at the local hospital. I enjoyed learning about the human body and about the different emergency lifesaving techniques. I'd already been promised a job upon completion of the course.

When I first started, I was very apprehensive en route to emergencies, but as time went on I felt more at ease. My first experience was a routine transfer from a general hospital to a psychiatric hospital. The total distance was about five miles. We weren't two miles from the hospital when I noticed the male patient wasn't breathing and I told the driver, "I think our patient is dead." I did what I could to revive him, but I honestly thought he had expired. The driver turned the rig around and headed back to the hospital. As we unloaded the patient, the driver checked the guy out and said to me, "I hope you are right." Minutes after we arrived and brought him into the emergency room, the doctor pronounced the elderly man dead. Everyone in the hospital was surprised because they realized we were transferring him to a psychiatric hospital, and we had just picked him up not even twenty minutes ago.

I was called out at all hours of the day and night. Some of the calls really affected me. A woman called and said her husband tried to commit suicide. We arrived at the scene and applied petroleum gauze to his chest. He had set an arrow on the inside of his garage and ran into it. He had a collapsed lung. I knew what it would take to be exactly where this man was psychologically, but I didn't talk to him too much. I just tried to reassure him that everything was going to be all right.

Another day, we received a call from the local police department about another suicide attempt. When we arrived we learned the husband was in his car, with it running, with the garage door shut. A family member called the police and as soon as the police arrived they opened the garage door and shut off the car. The man's face was blue and we immediately administered oxygen and transported him to the hospital. I felt the pain this man suffered also, because of my past experience with depression. I think God was using this job in my life to instill compassion in me, though at the time I wasn't aware of his plan for me.

One evening I was called at home to prepare myself to be picked up at the bottom of my driveway to respond to a nearby car accident. The driver picked me up within minutes after I received the phone call. My first question to the driver was, "What is the condition of the accident victims?" He said, "There was a head-on crash, three victims, two are critical, one with minor injuries." Our other ambulance was at the scene picking up the two victims who were listed critical because of massive head injures they sustained.

When we arrived at the scene we assisted the first ambulance crew, which took only a few minutes. I couldn't believe the condition of the two injured men. Just looking at their injures told you they were in a very serious state. I noticed the two cars: one was completely demolished, and in the other car the driver, just sitting there, was drunk. The drunken man slurred his words as I tried to talk to him. I bandaged up his small laceration and we loaded him on the stretcher and transported him to the hospital. In the emergency room, the two men were very unstable and were being transferred to a hospital with a state-of-the-art neurological department. I heard later on that one man expired and the other was still listed as critical. I realized at the time that the men were young–my age–in their late teens. How distraught I was to see this senseless destruction of human lives. I can still remember the accident as if it were yesterday, even though it happened thirty years ago.

When I look back at this accident, I thank God I never caused anyone injuries or death through my negligence. I remember how God protected my friend one day when we were hunting and the shotgun I was carrying went off just inches from his foot. My friend and I were so blessed by God's faithful protection. I know that there are consequences to sin, though I also know that the Lord Jesus Christ forgave me for my days of drinking and driving. I saw firsthand the terror, pain, and death that I could have caused.

One rainy Sunday, I received a call from the ambulance service dispatcher. She informed me I was to be picked up at my usual location, which was at a nearby store. I immediately hurried to get ready and headed out to meet the driver. It was only three miles away so it didn't take too long. The ambulance was waiting for me on the side of the road. When I got in my boss said to me, "What took you so long?" I told him I did my best, which usually wasn't good enough for him. He was a difficult boss, but I learned to persevere no matter what the trial or tribulation. He told me the accident was a bad one with two vehicles involved. The fire and police departments both were on site and they were using crowbars to extricate the victims. When we arrived I saw the mangled wreckage of both cars. In one of the cars, a woman appeared to be unconscious. After we pulled over and stopped, we ran over to check on her. We couldn't find a pulse and she wasn't breathing. She appeared to have broken her neck or back. My boss turned to me and said, "I think she's gone." We hurried over to the other vehicle. The occupants were a married couple in their fifties. The woman suffered with about a three-inch hematoma on her forehead, two broken wrists, and two broken ankles. The man was complaining about chest pain. They both had other minor bruises and were in shock.

We finally managed to place them on stretchers with the help of the fire and rescue crews, and soon we were off on our way to the hospital. As we left the accident scene, our other ambulance pulled up to pick up the young woman. I spoke to the driver briefly on the way and told him it was a tragedy what had happened to the pretty young woman in the other car. He agreed. I knew I needed to focus on the two people I was responsible for and treated them the best I could while we were en route to the hospital emergency room. We arrived at the hospital soon and brought the two people in.

After loading the stretchers back in the ambulance, we headed to pick up my car. On my way home I started to get upset. When I arrived home, the stress of the day hit me. I had never gotten so depressed from responding to an accident before. This one was the most difficult for me to handle.

I couldn't figure it out until recently with the help of the Holy Spirit. Again God was imparting His compassion and love into me for other people. His love is perfect, unconditional, and beyond what we could ever conceivably imagine. Yet He was still working with me, teaching me to love more and more.

Shortly after I arrived home, the telephone rang. It was the young woman's cousin. She told me her cousin was killed in an automobile accident that day. Now I was starting to get hysterical and frantically yelled out, "Where?" She said it was on the bridge that crosses the river. I practically dropped the phone. I was in tears. When she told me her name, I almost lost all composure. I told her I was at the scene today with the ambulance crew and picked up the occupants in the other car. I gave her my sincere condolences and thanked her for calling me. I had met her cousin months ago and we went out on a date. She was a kind person and was very thoughtful. We had a pleasant evening and I met her parents, who were very nice also. I was so upset about the woman's death that I couldn't work for the next two weeks. I called my boss at the ambulance company and said I was too upset to work right then. I apologized for the inconvenience. I told him I would keep him informed of my progress.

After I started back to work, I found it very difficult to perform my duties. Even though I have been healed from my fears and hurts through the blood of Jesus, certain memories would always be on my mind. This was a very difficult lesson for me to experience, just how very fragile life really is. In just a split second, we can be confronted with the judgment of God!

Chapter 14

Volunteer Firefighter

The weekly training at the fire station and also attending fire school at the state training facility was enjoyable training, but a lot different from actually being on the fire ground, though they try to make it seem authentic. I enjoyed the challenge that firefighting presents, along with the camaraderie among the men.

One day, just at nightfall, an alarm assignment came in over my fire department monitor. I rushed to respond to the call and finally arrived within ten minutes. Fire companies from other districts were responding. I immediately realized the status of the fire ground. Flames were roaring through one of the condominium units. I hurried to put on my turnout gear, my heart pounding and my adrenaline rushing.

As I was running over to report in, one of the engine company drivers told me that he was the first to arrive and had seen a woman in flames in a window. He was very upset about seeing her in the window, on fire and screaming for help. There was no way he could have been able to reach her on the second floor. It just wasn't possible. Sometimes though you realize the facts, you still feel helpless and saddened when it comes to people losing their lives. Finally, as other fire apparatus was being set up and more manpower arrived, we were in a better position to handle the blaze.

Though initially the fire was burning violently, it took only a short time to gain control of the blaze. We headed into the bedrooms next. The rooms smelled like a sweet perfume emanating from the burnt bodies. As we searched the unit, we found a woman's body and a few of us placed it into a body bag. I thought at that moment of what a terrifying way to die it must have been. I felt pity and compassion for her, yet I was still in disbelief concerning what had just transpired.

We walked into the adjacent bedroom and found her boyfriend next to the window lying on the floor. He apparently was trying to escape but couldn't make it. As soon as we placed him in a body bag, I knew it was time to go outside and assist with the cleanup by breaking down the ladders, hose lines, miscellaneous equipment, and by loading the trucks.

The fire was started by the woman's boyfriend, using gasoline as the accelerant to start the blaze. He doused the stairway, which was wood frame, and also his girlfriend. The man was apparently outraged over something and torched the building and set her on fire. The woman actually called the fire department dispatcher, screaming, "Help me! Help me!"

I couldn't understand how a person could hate a human being to the point of torching someone with gasoline. I was very sorrowful to see the destruction of both individuals, and how their lives were totally wasted in a matter of minutes. Being a part of this whole tragedy taught me a difficult lesson. I had never witnessed such a violent act upon another human being's life.

I think God was showing me just how distraught some people really are, and how badly they need to be taught about Jesus Christ. He is our deliverer and our shield in time of trouble. He is our only answer, the only way to the fullness of life, both mortal and immortal. "The Lord is my rock, and my fortress, and my deliverer; my God, my strength, in whom I will trust; my buckler, and the horn of my salvation, and my high tower" (Psalm 18:2). Once again He was imparting a deep compassion and love within me.

Compassion and love are the keys to tending to the needs of others. It's not about me. It's about Jesus. When we tend to the needs of others, we tend to the needs of Jesus Christ. "For I was hungered, and ye gave me meat, I was thirsty, and ye gave me drink: I was a stranger and ye took me in: Naked and ye clothed me: I was sick, and ye visited me: I was in prison, and ye came unto me. Verily I say unto you, Inasmuch as ye have done it unto one of the least of these my brethren, ye have done it unto me" (Matthew 25:35-36,40).

While traveling home in my car one afternoon, an engine company from another fire district in town crossed my path about one mile from my house. I quickly decided to follow the fire department to the call. On my way, I thought that it was just another false alarm because the district ended just ahead and routinely there were a number of false alarms at an apartment building nearby. I was determined to find out for myself.

I followed the engine company into the apartment building complex and could see flames emerging from one of the units' basement windows. I realized there was only one engine company arriving on the scene. I hurried to assist with connecting to the hydrant and ran over to check on the occupants. I noticed some of the tenants had their windows open and their units were filling up with smoke. To my right a elderly woman on the second floor was getting desperate. I told her not to worry—we would be taking care of her shortly. I ran over to the apparatus and with the help of another firefighter grabbed an extension ladder and quickly set the ladder up at the woman's window. I climbed up the ladder and talked to the woman about my intentions of bringing her down the ladder on my back. I explained the procedure and told her it was called a fireman's carry and reassured her that I would never let her fall and that I'd be with her until I got her safely on the ground where a stretcher was waiting for her. The smoke was getting worse in her room and I looked again into the hallway where I saw firefighters wearing air packs. I was concerned that she might have a heart attack and hoped that she would live through this whole ordeal. I knew I was just doing my job and reassured her that everything was going to be all right. I reached in and took her by the arm, then I had her safely held in place with her face looking straight down at the ground. I reassured her by telling her, as I climbed down the ladder, "A little more, a little more." Now my knees were shaking. It wasn't fire school training now. It was the real thing. I finally reached the ground, thank God. The ambulance crew was waiting for her and transported her to the hospital. The fire was eventually brought under control and extinguished, but many of the residents lost their homes for a period of time.

I believed God had directed me to follow the engine company. It was a split-second decision, and rare for me to respond to another fire department district's alarm without being called in. I think we all need to be available to do something for God's children. I thank God I have been able to reach out to people and care for them.

Chapter 15

Working for a Municipality

After working as an emergency medical technician for the ambulance service for a year, I decided to go back to work in a construction-related position. I applied at a number of construction companies and also at the public works department. Shortly after I applied, I received a call from the personnel office and was given a date to report to work. I was hired as a laborer, not having a clue about what the job entailed or what I was in for.

Once I started working with the crews, it didn't take me too long to get the picture. I was used to working very hard on the farm, construction work, and even on the ambulance crews, sometimes having to work around the clock.

When I started my new job, I was assigned to an underground fire alarm conduit installation, which was a major project. It took over three months to complete. After the conduits were installed and we pulled in the cable, I was assigned to assist the alarms supervisor with the cable connections, cut-over and removal of the old system.

My supervisors were angry with me because I was hired to work on the road crews and now I was being allowed to work in an area I enjoyed and was trying to better myself in. The men on the crews often complained because they said I worked too hard and made them look bad. My answer to them was to work hard and you won't have to worry about looking bad. On the other hand the supervisors were upset because I wasn't under their control every moment. It was one of those no-win situations.

Looking back I could have just quit, but I was becoming accustomed to trials and tribulations. God knew just what I needed, even though it hurt at times. "But we glory in tribulations also: knowing that tribulation worketh patience; and patience, experience; and experience, hope" (Romans 5:3b-4). Though at the time I didn't understand it, God was building me and molding me in patience, character, and hope. Though I thought it was a no-win situation, God was handling it, and He was making sure I would win and be able to give Him the glory.

For the most part it was a laid-back working environment. If the job didn't get done today, it would get done the next day, or the next week for that matter. It was hard for me to adapt to this routine because I was taught by my parents and previous employers to always do your best and always give a good day's work for the day's wages. There were a few men on the job who helped me and felt the same way as I did–that was a blessing that enabled me to handle the stress better.

As time progressed, I managed to get assigned permanently to the alarm department, where my supervisor became another challenge. The guys told me no one could ever work for him. At first I wondered why, but it didn't take too long to find out why. He never fully trained me to perform my duties. Sure, I graduated from trade school, but there were methods and techniques that you still needed to learn on the job and also various procedures. On the other hand, if something went wrong he'd say, "Why did that happen?" I think it was his way of maintaining a false sense of job security. Sometimes I thought he wanted me to work for him just for his convenience.

After working for the department for six months, our next big project was going to be working on the installation of a state-of-the-art alarm system. My job was to supervise and install a portion of the system. I was assigned a helper–and a helper he was not. I found him smoking marijuana one day and proceeded to tell him to never ever use drugs on the job again. He should have been fired, but I decided to give him another chance. It was another challenge working with someone who really didn't care about performing his duties to the best of his abilities. He, on the other hand, would do whatever the boss asked him to do, and it didn't matter if it was dishonest. Years later, the helper was fired for falsifying test records. I was taught to be honest no matter what the consequences.

The installations of the systems were difficult, but I continued to make progress. I couldn't figure out why my boss would tear my installations apart, looking for the smallest fault. He would even make up code violations to comfort his ego, and he wasn't even a licensed electrician. Still he would go on and on, picking at my workmanship. When it came to the contractors' work, nothing was ever said about their code violations. As a matter of fact, almost every site they worked on had to be reinstalled by another contractor to correct all their mistakes at the town's expense. I was amazed because an in-ground swimming pool was built at my boss's house, after he had just told me he was hurting for money a few months before. I didn't know what to think because many things that were going on were not right.

I needed to focus on my work, though, and on the Word of God, which teaches us: "For we know him that hath said, VENGEANCE BELONGETH UNTO ME, I WILL RECOMPENSE, saith the Lord. And again, The Lord SHALL JUDGE HIS PEOPLE" (Hebrews 10:30).

I went to people I thought I could trust and told them about the work having to be done over again, work which cost thousands and thousands of dollars. Some of them would never talk to me again about the subject once they checked on it. I was told by one town official not to bad-mouth the contractor, though I was just stating the facts about how poorly the system was installed and how the work violated the code. I knew I couldn't fight the system at the time, plus I was young. If the situation ever arises again, I thought, I would bring it to a Higher Authority, first to the Lord and ask for His direction, and then take it from there.

After spending five years in this work situation, I decided to put the whole experience behind me and start my own business. I called my boss on the two-way radio and asked him to meet me. He said, "I'll be free on Monday morning, or can you tell me on the radio"? I said no. It's not proper to discuss this issue over the radio.

He couldn't understand what the importance was but decided to call me on the telephone.

I told him on the phone that I had my letter of resignation for him. There was silence for a moment and then he told me I took him by surprise. If he only knew what I went through working for him all those years. The only reason I was able to withstand working with him was because God brought me through. I just didn't feel it was necessary to bring up the past though I would have liked to. He asked me who else knew about my leaving. I told him everyone who needed to know had been notified. His response was, "You know I'll be retiring shortly." I said, "You will be? That's good, but I'm leaving and thank you very much."

I saw him years later and he told me he still held the same position. I just couldn't continue to live my life around someone else's expectations. I didn't ever want to become like many of the people around me. When man is trying to mold you, it's impossible to live a free life. Man will put you in fear and bondage if you let him. When you allow yourself to be molded by Jesus Christ, He'll give you complete fullness of life and nurture you in His love. "The Lord is my light and my salvation; whom shall I fear? The Lord is the strength of my life; of whom shall I be afraid?" (Psalm 27:1).

Chapter 16

Married and
Bought the Farm

I thought I had met the woman of my dreams when a friend of mine introduced me to her girlfriend. We started dating and thought we loved each other so much that we decided to get married. Prior to our engagement, we discussed our faith in God and we reassured each other that we believed in God, the Bible, God's teachings, and also agreed to attend church services on Sunday. I thought that I had the comfort and security knowing that God would be at the center of our marriage.

We planned our wedding and were so excited with making the arrangements. It was a special time in our lives and everything turned out as planned, down to every detail. When I got married, I planned on being with my wife until the day I died.

On our way home from the airport, I brought up the subject of attending church the next Sunday. My wife answered me by saying, "I don't believe in God, and never did. I believe in the scientific explanation for the creation of man, just like my father." I said to her, "But what happened to your commitment to God you spoke to me about? You reassured me you believed in God." The only answer I got from her was, "Well I just don't believe."

At this point I felt our marriage was doomed. Marriages that are not equally yoked are very difficult to manage. "Be ye not unequally yoked together with unbelievers: for what fellowship hath righteousness with unrighteousness? and what communion hath light with darkness?" (2 Corinthians 6:14).

I was totally taken off guard and was in shock to think my wife could tell me her relationship with God was a huge lie. Her untruthfulness started to eat away at me, even though I tried to forgive her and reason with her. We started to argue then, and I was getting depressed and desperate.

When we finally arrived home, I walked out of the house in a rage. I took a walk and ended up at a small power substation just up the street from our house. The high-voltage power lines were low, and I thought about jumping up and grabbing them with my hand. Now I just wanted to end everything, no more lies and no more suffering. I would have been dead wrong though concerning suffering, my major sufferings would have just begun. "But the children of the kingdom shall be cast out into outer darkness: there shall be weeping and gnashing of teeth" (Matthew 8:12).

I decided to try my best at working out our major differences, but ended up separating myself from God. I started not attending church services, and we were both heading in the wrong direction. I didn't realize my wife was an alcoholic when I married her, and neither did she realize I was a workaholic. Two months before we were married, with the assistance of both our parents, we bought an eight-room Dutch Colonial.

The house was a handyman extra special. You name it, it needed it. We ended up installing new electrical wiring, plumbing, walls, ceilings, windows, doors, trim, moldings, carpeting, and paint inside and out. We built three new bathrooms, a laundry room and completely renovated the kitchen. We also had to cut down trees that were growing against the house and completely landscape the yard. The project took up almost all my time. It took intense labor and I appreciated my friends helping out with the major renovation project also. It was a lot of work but rewarding to see the finished product after all our efforts.

After spending many years working part time on the vegetable farm, the owner discussed his intentions with me concerning selling his property, which included about forty-two acres. Twenty acres of the land were tillable, and the remainder was wooded. The owner also leased eleven tillable acres. I told him I was interested in purchasing the parcel, but needed to see what my wife thought about the possibility. I talked to her about the property and told her the price was fair and that I could supplement our income by selling firewood off the land and by working on small electrical projects during the off-season. We both decided this would be a great business venture. The only problem was that she had no idea of the work involved to crop thirty-one acres of vegetables. I should have realized from the past that she was a good talker, but I didn't even consider her dishonesty. She told me she understood the many hours of work necessary to make this dream a reality.

We decided to purchase the property contingent upon our loan approval. I contacted a federal agency and consulted with the manager. We both went in for an initial visit to discuss the options of a low-interest government loan. The paperwork was quite involved, but we managed to conform to all their requirements. My wife had to quit her job because of our combined income being too much. If I had wisdom, I would have prayed about our whole plan and consulted with God. Once I found out my wife would have to quit her well-paying job; I should have said no thank you. I asked the agent if he could give us one year to get on our feet before she quit her job. He replied that it was impossible because of his rulebooks. The next requirement threw me–we were required to live on the farm or within a certain distance. Our remodeled home was less than five miles away from the property, but that wasn't close enough. Basically the agent told us we would have to build a new house on the new property. Right then and there I should have said no, but being young and immature, I just wanted to do my own thing and proceed with the impossible.

Finally, after waiting for three months, our loan was approved contingent on the sale of our house. Once our house was completed, which took a number of months, I called a man who had told me he was interested in purchasing it just after we bought it. He and his wife came over to look at it and liked it, but weren't ready to buy at the time. A few months later, they called our real estate agent and were serious about purchasing.

Meanwhile we had signed a contract with a real estate agent and were now required to pay a commission. At least that's what they told us at the time. The money we received paid off our mortgage with the bank and allowed us to place a substantial down payment on the farm property, which was used to pay for the construction of our new home.

Shortly following our spring closing, we broke ground for our house. I worked on the excavation, drainage, utilities, electrical wiring, plumbing, grading and landscaping. With the help of my friends, we made the necessary repairs on the tractors and other farm machinery, and I started tilling the ground for our first early corn crop. In the meantime, my wife convinced me to buy a horse for her. Even with everything else going on, I built a barn for the horse.

One day I decided to take the horse for a ride. Although I had experienced horseback riding when I was younger, I wasn't quite ready for the horse to take me for the ride of my life. The problem was that the horse had not been ridden very often, and once I got on, she took off and within minutes was out of control. She stopped just before a line of pine trees, ducked her head and sent me head first over her head and into the trees. It was a miracle that I wasn't even slightly injured.

It didn't take too long for my wife to lose interest in the whole process of working hard together, for the one common goal I thought we had set for ourselves to work as a team. She started drinking more and I started working more. Some nights I ended up working around the clock, while she ended up drinking at a local bar with friends, eventually arriving home intoxicated. When she got home, I'd ask her why she was drinking so much and told her she was hurting her body and it wasn't very thoughtful to drink just down the street from our house. Her response would be a filthy comment followed by verbal abuse. I hated seeing her drunk and listening to her anger.

By then, we had both been unfaithful to each other, which only made matters worse. From the start of our marriage, her lies had really torn me apart, and I felt hatred and confusion growing in me. The fact of her betraying me from day one didn't make it right for me to commit sin, which didn't accomplish anything other than letting the devil in for the kill. We attempted seeing a counselor to see if we could work out our differences, but we couldn't work it out without God. The one thing for sure was that there were going to be consequences to pay for our neglect of one another and for all our sins.

We were only able to operate the farm for two years due to financial difficulty. We ended up having to sell it in 1980 because the government raised our interest rate from three to twelve percent interest. The reason for the increase was because I needed to supplement our income by doing electrical work and when I was reviewed for the crop production for the year, I hadn't planted any crops because I didn't have any cash to work with. I didn't even have enough funds to purchase seed or vegetable bedding plants for the growing season. The agent said he was forced because of rules and regulations to implement the increase. There were other options available at the time. One idea was to subdivide a few lots to decrease the debt, but I didn't have a good advisor at the time and was probably too proud to ask my father for advice. There again I needed to seek God's face. We did sell one lot to help with our financial condition, but we should have worked out a viable plan.

Nevertheless, two years later in 1982, we were divorced. I didn't realize the effects of my divorce until months later. I realized then I had lost every ounce of my self-confidence down to the very last possible drop. I was drained emotionally, physically, spiritually, and financially. Where was I to turn?

God allowed me to come to the edge of disaster so that I would turn to Him. I guess this monumental conflict and disappointment is just what I needed to bring me back to Jesus Christ. I certainly had a lot of repenting to do and asked again to be forgiven of my sins, which I had committed. "If my people, which are called by my name, shall humble themselves, and pray, and seek my face, and turn from their wicked ways; then I will hear from heaven, and will forgive their sin, and will heal their land" (2 Chronicles 7:14).

One of my friends at the time was very helpful and concerned about me and stood by me during my divorce. My brother also came to my aid and spent hours talking with me, encouraging me, and was a big comfort and help to me. I knew from my past that giving up wouldn't have solved anything, and I recognized that my real source of strength was only going to come from God. "He giveth power to the faint; and to them that have no might he increaseth strength" (Isaiah 40:29).

Chapter 17

Business to Bankruptcy

One job I had held years earlier was with a communications business, installing mobile two-way radios and base-station antenna systems on buildings and towers. When I started getting serious about working solely at my own electrical business, I contacted a friend from my past at a communications company where I had worked. He was happy to hear from me and asked me to look over a project with him and give him a proposal. That one phone conversation led to an extensive contract with a utility company, which lasted for many years.

While I was at his office, the owner told me a local developer was looking for an electrician to work on his commercial properties. I called the developer the next day and arranged to meet with him. I ended up working as a subcontractor for him for five years and the work was quite steady. Whenever he had commercial electrical work, he called me to schedule my services.

I received a call from another developer and she advised me that one of my trade school instructors recommended me to wire her custom-built homes. As a matter of fact, shortly after receiving this call, the administrator at the school office called me and offered me a job teaching in the electrical department. I ended up owning and managing a construction, electrical, and communications business.

I spent over nineteen years working on various projects in different areas of the North East. I hired employees as necessary and hired many subcontractors to work on various projects. I enjoyed the hands-on portion of running my business the best. I also maintained a large inventory of supplies and miscellaneous equipment. God was blessing me so much through this period of my life that I should have stopped to think about what He was really doing and spent time with Him in prayer to show my appreciation.

God continued to protect me through very dangerous working environments. I worked on high tower structures for power and communications networks, in deep underground tunnels, excavations, blasting and road-building projects, operated heavy construction machinery in close proximity to underground and overhead hazards, installed high-amperage battery plants, high-voltage power systems, overhead fire-alarm networks. I worked in various nuclear, hydroelectric, oil, and coal generating plants and worked in many high-voltage substations. God has always been faithful looking over my crews and myself.

Another thing I failed to do was to continue to thank and praise God. I also didn't seek His instruction nor the counsel of a financial planner. I had so many blessings in my life but I needed to seek God fully. "I will instruct thee and teach thee in the way which thou shalt go: I will guide thee with mine eye" (Psalm 32:8). You would think by then that I would have been able to trust God and fully turn to Him in time of need and stick by Him. But there were still lessons I needed to learn and I ended up learning them the hard way.

My business took off and involved hard work and a countless number of dedicated hours. The money was pouring in like water flowing from an endless well. Actually I spent the money even before I received it. I had a high line of credit and could buy just about anything, either on the credit line or with plastic. I didn't stop to realize the water line, which was fed from the well, could go dry. Though I spent money on heavy equipment, trucks, machinery, and tools, I always thought it was okay because I was putting the revenue back into the business. How wrong I was! My financial disaster was about to erupt.

Another major mistake I made was purchasing an old home at a very exorbitant price, thinking the work would always be there. The contracts I held at the time were very lucrative, so I went for it, with the help of my friends telling me it was a good investment.

I was wrong again. I had already remodeled a house for very little money, and built a new house at a nominal cost. Now I purchased a home for double what it would have cost me to have built it myself. My reasoning at the time was that I was so busy that I didn't have the time to build one. To make life simpler I should have just moved into an apartment. One of my huge faults through the years was that I lacked wisdom. "If any of you lack wisdom, let him ask of God, that giveth to all men liberally, and upbraideth not; and it shall be given him" (James 1:5).

Time was progressing now. My contract with my major client, which involved working forty to sixty hours per week, was being cut back to hardly eight hours, and it didn't take too long for the contract to be terminated. All it took was a new director in charge with no interest in new projects, and I was finished.

I realized years before that I shouldn't have put my eggs in one basket and did try to market my talents and abilities to other companies, but I was so busy with my main client that I never pursued too much other work. Because of my huge loss in revenue, I couldn't afford my large mortgage payments any longer.

I decided to move out and turn the house over to the mortgage company. I didn't realize at the time that there was bankruptcy protection I could have filed for to keep the house. Also a refinance company was interested in working with me initially, but I contacted them too late for them to proceed. At the time, I planned on giving the majority of my business equipment and personal household furnishing to foreign missions. When I arrived at the mission's office, I learned that a ministries group in Liberia, Africa had been praying for the various equipment and supplies I was leaving off. "Every man according as he purposeth in his heart, so let him give; not grudgingly, or of necessity: for God loveth a cheerful giver" (2 Corinthians 9:7).

I was pleased that God enabled me to assist the people who had so diligently been praying for the equipment. Praise God again for his faithfulness!! Finally after two months I had everything cleaned out of my rental space that I had accumulated over the nineteen years I was in business. I was relieved and expecting a much easier lifestyle working for an employer rather than being self-employed. After working a number of years and trying to pay off the debts I incurred while in business, I had no other choice but to file bankruptcy.

It was a difficult decision to make, and little by little God was showing me that He was my priority, not things of this world. "Lay not up for yourselves treasures upon earth, where moth and rust doth corrupt, and where thieves break through and steal: But lay up for yourselves treasures in heaven, where neither moth nor rust doth corrupt, and where thieves do not break through nor steal: For where your treasure is, there will your heart be also" (Matthew 6:19-21).

Chapter 18

My Lovely Christian Wife and Son

My wife and I met through another girl I was dating at the time. The girl I was introduced to was named Laura. At that time, Laura was in the process of getting a divorce. Even though it wasn't the greatest timing to start dating, I was willing to give it a try. Once I laid my eyes on her, I realized that this was the woman of my dreams. I was strategically thinking how I'd find out about her with my girlfriend right there.

It was a very uncomfortable situation, even though my girlfriend and I weren't getting along too well at the time. We were having a hard time compromising with each other, among other things, and it just wasn't working out. I came up with a crazy question and said to Laura, "Where do you get your hair cut?" What could her answer possibly do for me? But it was just the ticket. She answered me by saying, "My girlfriend cuts my hair at my house." I proceeded to ask her if I could get my hair cut by her friend, and she said yes.

I was relieved now that I was going to get the opportunity to see her again. I was really determined to get to know her. I got directions to her mother's house and had my hair cut, but at the same time I couldn't keep my eyes off of Laura. It was love at first sight. I just flipped over her, because she was sincere, had a heart for people, was gorgeous, intelligent, motivated, affectionate, and to sum it all up, a true blessing.

After our visit at her home, I called her and we agreed to meet. At first Laura didn't want to become involved. She was still hurting and waiting for her divorce to be settled. Of course I wanted to be the hero who would relieve her of the pain and misery she was experiencing. I tried to chill out and give her the space she needed. I always hated the phrase, "I need space." When women would use that line on me, I would say okay, grumble and complain for a while, and then start dating someone else.

With Laura something was different, and I knew I needed to wait it out. Finally, after a couple of weeks, we started dating quite often. It had only been a two-week wait but it seemed like months. It didn't take very long for Laura and me to start getting very serious.

Two months later, we traveled to a house in the mountains to spend the weekend. We ended up having the best time of our lives, spending time together. The more I was with her the more I wanted to spend every moment I could with her. She was interested in my life, my desires, and my needs. We started doing everything together and fell deeply in love with each another. Months later she had a change in her menstrual cycle and went to see her doctor. The doctor took a pregnancy test and it turned out to be positive. We knew the situation we were in wasn't consistent with the Word of God and neither was it proper. But Laura and I felt so blessed and happy to know that we were going to have a baby.

As time progressed we were so excited to have made the commitment to have our child. Laura looked even more beautiful pregnant. She would just glow with a happiness and love that had to have been from God. I admired not only her appearance but also her heart to love, her compassion, and positive personality. Laura continued with her routine doctor's visits, and we went together some of the time. When her appointment was scheduled for the ultrasound, we were so excited with the thought of seeing our baby in her womb. When we viewed the ultrasound image, our baby's legs were apart and the nurses told us the baby was in a perfect position to determine we were having a boy, no doubt. It was a thrill to see our baby forming and to see that he was a boy. We would be blessed whether we had a boy or a girl.

We planned our wedding in the middle of all our preparations. We invited our immediate family and were blessed to come together in matrimony. We had a small, intimate, and special gathering. Laura and I were now husband and wife. We were married by a justice of peace, and we all enjoyed the celebration.

As time went on, my wife and doctor agreed on a date for her to be admitted into the hospital to give birth to our child. When Laura was ten days past her due date, the doctor recommended that labor be induced. After she was settled in, the nurse gave her the initial medication to induce her. She immediately started to experience contractions, cramping, and pain. The next day she was given an epidermal because of the severe pain. The nurse asked me to leave the room. The next thing I heard was my wife screaming from the end of the corridor. I was terrified to hear her in such agonizing pain. Then the doctor gave her a second epidural because the first wasn't effective.

The next day at the hospital she pushed for three and a half hours and found out the baby wouldn't fit through her birth canal. The doctor came in from time to time and would say, "Just a little while longer." The nurses, doctor, and I coached Laura, and we all tried our best. Laura's labor was soon to reach over thirty-three hours. When the doctor came in to make his rounds, he told my wife again, "Just a little while longer." Well at this point she had had enough and screamed, "I am not waiting any longer. You are going to operate." The doctor was so pleasant and said, "Okay, we'll get everything ready." My wife said, "Do what you have to do and get going." The nurse asked if I was going in the operating room. We had already consulted with each other and decided we would stay together through the procedures. The only glitch was that Laura would only be given local anesthesia if I were present in the operating room.

Time was mounting up now, and we were increasingly concerned about our baby's health. The nurse handed me the clothing to be worn in the operating room along with a mask and told me to get ready right away. The anesthesiologist instructed me to stay seated during the procedure until our baby was born. I obeyed him until our son was born, then I jumped up and looked in amazement at how absolutely beautiful he looked. I was so proud and happy. I had never witnessed anything so beautiful and special as the birth of our son Tommy. Immediately after his birth, they checked his vital signs, cleansed him, wrapped him in a blanket and handed our son to me. I was so excited when I showed our newborn son to my lovely wife, Laura. We were truly blessed and happy to receive God's gift to both of us, a miracle, a new life.

After my holding the baby for a short period, the nurse needed to take him into the nursery. I was reluctant at first but then said okay and turned Tommy over to the nurse. Then it hit me that my camera with fresh film was sitting on the windowsill in the operating room. During all the excitement, I forgot to take any photos and was a little disappointed. Then I thought I should be thankful and joyful because our son was born healthy. Thank you Jesus!

Laura was brought into her room soon after the birth, and we greeted each other with a big kiss and huge hug. We were absolutely thrilled about our son's birth. The nurse brought him in periodically for his feedings and we loved being with him every second. After Laura's hospital stay, which was seven days, we made the necessary preparations and bundled Tommy up for the ride home. It was a new experience for all three of us. I was very fortunate at the time to be able to take almost two months off from work. For a change, I was able to spend quality time and fully care for them. We received many calls from friends and family congratulating us on our new member to the family. Laura and I again thanked God for our healthy son. My wife and our son are such a major blessing and very special to me. They bring so much more joy into my life. "These things have I spoken unto you, that my joy might remain in you, and that your joy might be full" (John 15:11).

Chapter 19

Accepting Jesus Christ as My Savior

While my wife Laura was having lunch at a restaurant one day, she started talking to another woman who was there with her children. After chatting for a while, about different topics and also about Jesus, Laura was asked to stop by the woman's house to visit. When Laura arrived at her house, the woman called her pastor to see if Laura could meet him.

My wife met the pastor at his church and he shared about the life of Jesus. He asked Laura if she wanted to accept Jesus as her Savior and she accepted him without hesitation. Subsequently my wife and son started attending a spirit-filled Christian church. Months went by and each Sunday my wife would say to me: "Dear, it's time for us to go to church. Would you like to come with us?" Every Sunday my answer was: "It's great you and Tommy are going to church but I am all set for now." I was brought up Catholic and always thought I was all set. The truth of the matter was that I had never fully committed my life to Jesus Christ.

Months later the church started organizing a Christmas program that was being performed by the children. Tommy was going to be in the play. I was invited by Tommy and Laura to attend. Of course Daddy was going to attend an event in which his son was going to perform. A month later we all got ready and were excited to go together as a family to share this special occasion. The evening was filled with excitement. Watching our dear son in the program was very special.

God, on the other hand, had something even more awesome to offer. Toward the end of the program the pastor announced it was time for prayer. I thought, okay, a short prayer and then the evening will come to a close.

The pastor presented an invitation for anyone who hadn't accepted Jesus as their personal Savior to be able to. I understood that we can't earn our salvation; we are saved by the grace of God. "For by grace are ye saved through faith: and that not of yourselves: it is the gift of God" (Ephesians 2:8). He went through the steps of salvation, one by one, and I recited a prayer after him, "That If thou shalt confess with thy mouth the Lord Jesus, and shalt believe in thine heart that God hath raised him from the dead, thou shalt be saved. For with the heart man believeth unto righteousness; and with the mouth confession is made unto salvation" (Romans 10:9-10).

I felt heaven open up as I proclaimed Jesus Christ as my Lord and Savior over my life. I started weeping and became so on fire for Christ. "The spirit itself beareth witness with our spirit, that we are the children of God" (Romans 8:16). At the age of forty-one, in December of 1993, I accepted Jesus Christ as my Savior. Laura and I received Jesus because of a stranger at a restaurant expressing her faith in boldness and love for Jesus Christ. "And blessed is he, whosover shall not be offended in me" (Matthew 11:6). I believe it was all part of God's plan for us. We serve a merciful and loving God.

Laura has been used powerfully by bringing the spirit of song into my life. After receiving Jesus Christ, her songs were ignited and transformed into spiritual songs of praise and adoration to our Lord and Savior.

Something else took place when I took the step of accepting Jesus. Laura and I started attending church with our son on Sunday. We spent two years at that church where we had accepted Jesus. Laura became a member of the worship ministry. I was excited to find out that the church was going to move to a new location where I'd be able to assist with the renovation work. I became immediately involved with the project and spent many hours enjoying the labor and some tasks of fixing up our new church home with my brothers and sisters in Christ. Finally the project was completed and our Sunday services commenced in our new building. I was blessed to have been part of God's plan and vision for the community.

My wife and I were grateful to the pastor who led us to Christ, and we became good friends with his family. They are sincere, faithful, and loving people. We also enjoyed our fellowship with them and with the congregation. After a number of years, our pastor and his family transferred to another church. He and his family were true servants, and now it was time for them to move on. Laura and I were disappointed, along with many other people, but we knew it was for the best and we certainly wanted the best for them.

Months later we visited them in the state of New York for a weekend. Their church family was holding a tent meeting, and a group from Integrity Music was playing. It was a powerful experience of praising and worshiping the Lord. We gathered together in the pastor's home after the service and enjoyed lunch and fellowship with the music ministry crew. Later on in the day we got together at the pastor's home with his family. The presence of God's joy fell upon us and we continued to laugh for what seemed like hours. The word of God tells us, "For the joy of the Lord is your strength" (Nehemiah 8:10). We experienced such joy and had a wonderful time in the powerful presence of God.

Once our pastor transferred to his new location, our church body started searching for a new pastor and was experiencing growing pains. Not having a leader in the church was a challenge, and I saw firsthand how jealousy and envy can operate, even in the midst of a Christian body. The devil doesn't care who you are. He's always seeking to destroy. "Be sober, be vigilant; because your adversary the devil, as a roaring lion, walketh about, seeking whom he may devour" (1 Peter 5:8).

It was now time for my family to move on. I searched for an answer from God and He made His answer very plain and simple where we were to go. I had assisted a maintenance man with repairs at a nursing home where my brother was the administrator. We became friends almost immediately with his wife and their family. When he was sick, I visited him at home and at the hospital when he was brought in, which was quite often. After a very long and difficult sickness, he went home to the Lord. Laura and I were introduced to our new church at my friend's funeral service. "For my thoughts are not your thoughts, neither are your ways my ways, saith the Lord" (Isaiah 55:8).

The love of Christ just emanated through the atmosphere of the church. It was an awesome manifestation of the Holy Spirit's presence and peace. I found myself upset that I had lost a friend, but I was reassured by experiencing this powerful service that my friend was now in the hands of God. Being a witness to the awesome presence of God also has enlarged my faith in Him.

I turned to my friend, who now was a widow, and told her the service was beautiful and the presence of God so strong. She wanted us to meet her pastor. Following the service she introduced my wife and me to the pastor and his wife. They made us feel at home from that point on.

We initially started attending the church services during the weekdays. I continued to pray about God's will concerning the church we were to attend. Two weeks later God made it clear where he was leading us. Friends asked us if we were sure about the change, and I assured them God was doing the leading. "I will instruct thee and teach thee in the way which thou shalt go: I will guide thee with mine eye" (Psalm 32:8).

We experienced positive growth in our new church. My wife continued to minister on the worship team and we both absolutely loved worshiping the Lord. The people accepted our family, and I was so thankful to God for bringing us to our new church home.

During one service while I was praising God with my hands reaching out to God, He touched my right hand. I said, "Yes, Lord!" God led me to the front of the church, and right then I knew in my spirit God had something for me to say. The presence of the Holy Spirit was so strong I was ready to fall out. I spoke out to the congregation saying, "As we reach out to the Lord, He will grasp our hand, lead us, and fill us with His love and peace." I felt so full of God's presence, and when our pastor came over to lay hands on me to pray, I immediately fell out from the power of God. I just love the presence of God. "Draw nigh to God, and he will draw nigh to you" (James 4:8).

One Sunday the worship team needed a drummer. I had played the drums when I was younger but never really in a group. I would play for hours listening to rock music and really didn't understand the lethal content of the music I was playing. We shouldn't be deceived by the devil's devices. I should have never listened to secular rock music because it is deceiving and it could have led me totally away from God. When one of the deacons came over to me in church and asked me to play the drums on the worship team, I was reluctant to say yes because I had limited experience playing them. What I didn't know at the time was that by saying no I would have been limiting what God had planned for me. My answer to him was, "Oh! You need a drummer?" Then the deacon said, "You'd better go up and play. We need you." I asked him to help me set them up and he told me to do it myself. The reason I asked him for help was because I was very embarrassed. For many years I had been intimidated easily from the lack of confidence my divorce from my first marriage instilled in me.

When I turned beet red and started sweating, some people would think it was a joke, laugh and say,"Hey, you're red." People are people, I would always say, and sometimes will only change when God directs them. When I turned red and started sweating bullets in front of the church family setting up the drums, no one in the church made a negative comment about it to me. It was a good change for me and I felt blessed. The worship leader gave me a few pointers as we progressed. I finally was able to concentrate on the Lord and seek His presence and direction during the service. This was God's initial plan to free me from the bondages of intimidation, embarrassment, and fear. I had asked God to deliver me, and from stepping out in faith I was taking back what the devil had stolen from me. The whole process took a number of months to complete, but when I was needed to play the drums, little by little I was being set free. "For God hath not given us the spirit of fear; but of power, and of love, and of a sound mind" (2 Timothy 1:7).

Chapter 20

Marriage Counselor

After being married for a while, my wife and I decided to consult a counselor. I don't recommend that anyone seek a counselor of different Christian beliefs or values. The minister was a dear man and he directed us to various scriptures to back up his lectures with us, but in some areas there was untruth associated with his interpretation of the Word of God. He told us that if we were to die today, our spirit would hover over our bodies and we wouldn't be with Christ until His second coming. He also told us we weren't allowed to eat certain meats. We not only were counseled by this minister, but he also invited us to attend his church, which we did on Saturdays for a period of time. This definitely wasn't the will of God.

We had many counseling sessions with him and his main focus was directed toward each of us circumcising our flesh and becoming one flesh. "FOR THIS CAUSE SHALL A MAN LEAVE HIS FATHER AND MOTHER, AND SHALL BE JOINED UNTO HIS WIFE, AND THEY TWO SHALL BE ONE FLESH" (Ephesians 5:31), which is easier said than done. He pointed out to me that maybe God was using my wife to purify me. I didn't peculiarly like the idea but he definitely had a point.

I quickly started to learn that if I didn't like the little things my wife did or did not do, I needed to stop complaining and do something about it myself. For example, I complained for months to myself and to Laura about having to do the laundry and dishes after a hard day's work. The proper way of managing this problem would have been to pray about it and then discuss it with my wife.

I omitted the most important part, which was to bring it to the Lord in prayer, and would just jump into a discussion, which led nowhere. After complaining over and over again, God gave me the solution I wasn't necessarily looking for when He said: "You do the laundry and dishes."

As always when God spoke to me, He knew exactly what He was telling me to do. My part of His plan was to become a better listener and take His directives to heart and act on them immediately. One evening the Lord told me: "Love your wife for my glory." When I heard the word "glory," God's powerful presence fell upon me, which I just love. Shortly after I heard His request, I turned to the scripture: "Husbands, love your wives, even as Christ also loved the church, and gave himself for it" (Ephesians 5:25).

He didn't say to me, love your wife and I'll check in with you in a couple of years to check on your results. He directs us in Scripture quite plainly by saying: "I WILL NEVER LEAVE THEE, NOR FORSAKE THEE" (Hebrews 13:5). He is always with us to shepherd His people, which we see by the examples set forth in the Word of God. Jehovah-Rohi, our God and Shepherd. "The Lord is my shepherd; I shall not want" (Psalm 23:1). "I am the good shepherd, and know my sheep, and am known of mine" (John 10:14).

I've been guilty of saying that I'm getting sick of having to give in to my wife. Isn't it time for her to start changing? The answer I've always gotten from God is that I am the one who needs to change, and love my wife in the process. Of course that wasn't the answer I was looking for, but the answer God was using to humble me. As soon as I got down on my knees and sincerely prayed for the Holy Spirit to help, God took over and made the biggest positive difference in my life. "But we will give ourselves continually to prayer, and to the ministry of the word" (Acts 6:4).

Sometimes the smallest disturbance in our marriage turned into a major fiasco. When we learned to turn to God to fight our battles, we experienced a new way of dealing with our problems. The difference with God was that He fought our battles with His love and we recognized He was in the very center of our lives and marriage. I'll never forget the night God spoke to me and said: "I live in your wife. When you talk to her you are also talking to me. "Hereby know we that we dwell in him, and he in us, because he hath given us of his spirit" (1 John 4:13).

The Holy Spirit was teaching me to act in the character of God, who is love. When I see a needy person on the street, I no longer turn my back on him or her but offer some assistance, even if it's a matter of giving someone my Bible, my coat, a meal, or a drink of water.

After two months, one of our Christian sisters from our Spirit-filled church visited us at home. When I answered the door and welcomed her in, she told us God spoke to her and told her to go and visit us. She talked with us, shared the following scriptures and explained them: "For though I be absent in the flesh, yet am I with you in the spirit, joying and beholding your order, and the steadfastness of your faith in Christ" (Colossians 2:5). We learned that when our mortal body dies, we are given an immortal body and are immediately present with our Lord Jesus Christ. The next scripture was found in Colossians 2:16: "Let no man therefore judge you in meat, or in drink, or in respect of a holyday, or of the new moon, or of the sabbath days."

Clearly the Word indicates the truth concerning meat, which being interpreted means food. We are not bound by any law regarding the consumption of food. These were good lessons learned in seeking the face of God and His truth, which are clearly found in the Word of God. We immediately got back on track because of our sister's obedience to God.

When we returned to our church where we both accepted Jesus Christ as our Savior, our pastor and his wife were so happy to see us and welcomed us back with open arms. My wife and I were filled with the spirit of peace when we returned to our Spirit-filled Christian church once again. "These things I have spoken unto you, that in me ye might have peace" (John 16:33).

Chapter 21

Chest Pain

At times in my marriage, I thought I needed peace and quiet. I'd say to Laura and Tommy, "I need rest. Don't you understand?" What I really needed to do was to get on my knees and pray, praise, trust and be thankful to God for all He had done, was doing and for His entire plan for my family. "Trust in the Lord with all thine heart; and lean not unto thine own understanding. In all thy ways acknowledge him, and he shall direct thy paths" (Proverbs 3:5-6).

One night both of them continued to knock on the bedroom door when I was trying to sleep. I kept pleading with them to let me rest, and then I started to get angry. Before I knew it, I started to experience pains in my chest.

This was the beginning of a stressful ordeal because I didn't take the whole situation and circumstance to Christ. I yelled down the stairs to Laura that I was experiencing chest pain, she called 911, and within minutes an ambulance arrived along with the fire and police departments.

They immediately took my vital signs, administered oxygen, placed me on a stretcher, and loaded me in the ambulance. Soon we arrived at a nearby hospital. Laura took Tommy to a neighbor to watch him and then drove to the hospital. Once I arrived at the hospital, the doctor ordered the usual tests for someone in my condition.

After all the tests, I was told my heart looked okay but was advised to follow up with a stress test as soon as possible. I immediately made an appointment with a cardiologist and arranged for a visit.

During my office visits, I was allowed to pray for patients, thanks to my doctor's love for Jesus. He took an electrocardiogram and said it appeared fine. He prescribed a tranquilizer, which I was hesitant to take because of my past experience, but at least the dose was mild. Next he scheduled a stress test at the local hospital. The first test went well, but the second one showed a spot in my heart during the scanning that was done. The doctor advised me the only way to ensure my heart was healthy and to put my mind at ease was to have an angiogram performed. He explained what he would do and said there was a possibility I could die during the procedure. I thought and prayed about it for a few days and then called him to schedule an appointment. I really needed to know the condition of my heart and was eager to get this behind me.

I was quickly admitted as an outpatient at the hospital, medicated, and brought into the procedure room. The doctor explained each step and procedure, but when he made the incision on my femur I felt faint and was nauseous. My blood pressure dropped due to my anxiety. He said we'll give you some medication to help you out, and after a few minutes I felt better. I watched the monitor as the wire traveled through my heart. Next he injected a dye, and I was amazed at how clear the picture was. Though it was awesome, I couldn't wait for the procedure to be completed.

My prognosis was excellent. My doctor advised me that my heart was in good condition and he was not worried about it at all. The chest pain I had experienced was associated with overexertion and stress. I was now able to relax, knowing I didn't have a heart condition. I learned to manage my stress better. "It is of the Lord's mercies that we are not consumed, because his compassions fail not. They are new every morning: great is thy faithfulness" (Lamentations 3:22-23).

Chapter 22

Childlike Faith

One evening Laura and I made plans to go out to dinner. The evening was going to be totally in God's hands, because I had just completed a forty-day fast on bread and water, and I knew God had something special planned for our evening together.

Finally we left for our date and arrived at the first restaurant. God had directed me to stop at a restaurant to see if a particular waitress was working whom I had been trying to witness to. If she was working, we were to have dinner there. If she wasn't working, we were to have dinner across the street at another restaurant.

We went in and found out the waitress wasn't working. So I told Laura that it was time to leave. She hesitated and said, "What are you doing?"

I said, "God has a plan tonight. Just bear with me and you will see." We got in our car and drove to the next restaurant's parking lot.

We gave the hostess our name and she told us we would have a short wait. By now my wife was wondering if I needed to see a doctor. While we were waiting for our table, Laura and I talked about how the Lord was leading me. I told her something was going to happen. Still puzzled, she was wondering what I meant. I told her that I didn't know for sure what was going to happen, but that we'd just have to wait and see.

After only ten minutes, the hostess called us and seated us at a quiet corner table. Both of us were so happy to be out spending some quality time together. Shortly after we sat down, the waitress came over and discussed the specials and menu with us. By the time she took our order, my wife and I were talking, laughing, and enjoying each other's company. It wasn't long before our salads were brought to the table. We joined hands and prayed together for God to bless our family, our meal, and for His plan and will to be accomplished that night.

After taking just a few bites of food, we were interrupted by a disturbance at the table right next to ours. A middle-aged man about six feet tall was pounding on a woman's shoulder blades with the palm of his hand. As he continued to hit her, I was surprised he didn't break her back. I immediately got up to see if I could possibly help and noticed she was choking on some food. My first thought was to use the Heimlich method, but God spoke the words to me: "Pray for her."

I rushed over and put my hand on her arm and started speaking in tongues out loud. I looked up and Laura was praying in tongues also. We both continued to pray, believing God was going to move on the woman's behalf. By now the man had stopped pounding on the woman's shoulders also. Within seconds a piece of meat shot out of the woman's mouth. Shortly after that, we stopped praying and said, "Thank you, Jesus." I told the woman that Jesus had taken care of her tonight even though she didn't seem the least bit interested in what had miraculously taken place by His power and authority.

Next, I asked her if she was finished with her meal, took her plate to the kitchen and returned to our table and thanked Jesus for saving the woman's life. By then the other people in the restaurant who had stopped talking and eating were getting back into their routines as if nothing had ever happened.

Our conversation for the remainder of the evening focused around how special and faithful God really is. Laura and I wondered if the woman fully realized what the Lord actually had done for her that night. In Exodus 15:26, the Word of God teaches us: "For I am the Lord that healeth thee." We serve such a powerful, faithful, and loving God, Praise you Jesus!!

I shared this story with relatives who told me, "If I'm choking, use the Heimlich method first, then pray for me second." But I know one thing for sure, and that is that God needs to always come first.

As we prepared to leave the parking lot, we noticed a motor vehicle accident had just occurred in front of the restaurant. I pulled over and ran up to the car to see if I could offer any assistance. I went over to the woman who was sitting in the passenger seat of the damaged car, She appeared to be in shock and asked if I could pray for her. I started praying. I asked God to heal her and fill her with peace. Then I felt the presence of Jesus. She was hesitant about having the ambulance take her to the hospital, and I suggested the best thing she could do would be to get checked out by the professionals at the hospital. Her question to me was, "Who are you?" I told her I was a friend of Jesus and was concerned about her. I had just finished talking with her when a police officer came up to me and politely asked me if I was all set. I said, "Yes, I'm ready to leave," and he assisted me by directing me into the traffic.

Driving home, Laura and I praised and thanked God for leading us. "Be thou exalted, O God, above the heavens; let thy glory be above all the earth" (Psalm 57:5).

Chapter 23

Visitation and Deliverance from God

One evening after reading part of a book entitled *Good Morning, Holy Spirit*, by Benny Hinn, I felt inspired after reading the chapter, "Knowing God's Presence." The author described his first powerful encounter with the Holy Spirit, which he described as an unusual breeze, like a wave moving over him. I went to bed and awoke at 2:00 A.M. I walked into the bathroom and as I contemplated asking the Holy Spirit to move in my life, He surely did.

At first it felt like electrical impulses in my head, and then the Holy Spirit sent fire through my body into my feet. It lasted for twenty minutes. For a number of months, I had asked God to deliver me from the bondages of unclean and confusing thoughts. I believed God would answer my prayers to give me freedom from these issues, and I continued to wait upon the Lord for months. "Wait on the Lord: be of good courage, and he shall strengthen thine heart: wait, I say, on the Lord" (Psalm 27:14).

I asked God to take away everything that was not of Him because I didn't want to be burdened with it. As day after day turned into weeks and months, all this time I prayed for deliverance. "And all things, whatsoever ye shall ask in prayer, believing, ye shalt receive" (Matthew 21:22). This particular evening I was going to ask the Holy Spirit for a supernatural touch of deliverance, but before I could get the words out of my mouth He started His work in me. "For your Father knoweth what things ye have need of, before ye ask him" (Matthew 6:8). I happily received everything that God was pouring into my life. I was so on fire my feet felt like the flames of a torch. The purifying fire of the Holy Spirit took place every evening for a month when I went to bed and lasted for ten to twenty minutes or so.

While I was lying in bed, the Holy Spirit sent a supernatural electrical frequency that sent surges of power from the top of my head to the soles of my feet. I would also experience spasms in my muscles that would make my whole body shake. God was performing a purifying work of fire in me. Finally after a season of expecting and believing, I was delivered. "Then flew one of the seraphims unto me, having a live coal in his hand, which he had taken with the tongs from off the altar: And he laid it upon my mouth, and said, Lo, this hath touched thy lips; and thine iniquity is taken away, and thy sin purged" (Isaiah 6:6-7).

Chapter 24

Familiar Spirits of the Enemy

Shortly after the Lord spoke to me concerning writing this book, the devil decided to attack me with deceiving familiar spirits. His main thrust was an attempt to attack my pride. The devil showed me many dreams and spoke to me through them. He spoke to me quite often and tried to deceive me into believing I was hearing from God. Once he accomplished this first step, the sky would have been the limit and he would have moved in for the kill.

The experience I've received from this type of warfare has enabled me to minister to people and to better understand the deception of the enemy. The only real way to conquer an enemy is to study his tactics and to be one step ahead of him. "Be sober, be vigilant; because your adversary the devil, as a roaring lion, walketh about, seeking whom he may devour" (1 Peter 5:8).

My dreams were generated from hell, though one might not think so.

Jesus was tempted by the devil in the wilderness and also in the holy city at the Temple (Matthew 4:1,5). The devil tempted Jesus, and there is no reason why he wouldn't try to deceive me with his lies, for he is the father of lies. "He was a murderer from the beginning, and abode not in the truth, because there is no truth in him. When he speaketh a lie, he speaketh of his own: for he is a liar, and the father of it" (John 8:44b).

I have listed a few examples of the devil's deceiving dreams below:

- *Maintain a farm in Iowa and harvest thousands of acres of wheat*

- *Build a machinery repair building, and a building for the employees*
- *Build two twenty-four-thousand-square-foot warehouses*
- *Build a church, a school, and six houses for the staff*
- *Purchase various trucks, construction and farm equipment*

At the time I didn't know what to think, but I quickly learned the truth. One evening our family was invited to a dear Christian family's house for dinner. Both our families gathered around the table before dinner to praise and pray to the Lord. I started to share about my dreams.

My friend interrupted me immediately and said: "That is not God." He shared a story with us about one of his friends. His friend had shared the same kind of lies from the devil that I had just shared. The man started feeling like a robot because the devil was ordering him around frequently. The man had a heart attack and died because of the stress. All along the man thought it was God directing him. I had already started feeling like a robot myself, because the devil was using the same tactics on me and trying to infiltrate my life completely.

I called another dear Christian and shared the same dreams. She said to me: "I don't get a witness about what I am hearing. Put it on the back burner for now, continue to pray and seek the face of God in your life. God will definitely lead you."

Now I had confirmation. The truth was that the attack was coming from the devil and his demons in the form of familiar spirits, even though the dreams were in color and everything looked so real. I needed to act on God's voice and not on the voice of a stranger. "My sheep hear my voice, and I know them, and they follow me" (John 10:27).

If I had listened to the enemy concerning all his deception, I possibly could have built myself up with a false sense of pride. In 1 Peter 5:5, the Bible teaches us, "GOD RESISTETH THE PROUD, AND GIVETH GRACE TO THE HUMBLE," and goes on to say in 1 Peter 5:6, "Humble yourselves therefore under the mighty hand of God, that He may exalt you in due time."

Chapter 25

Ishmael Trip

Part 1

Sarai said unto Abram, Behold now the Lord hath restrained me from bearing: I pray thee, go in unto my maid; it may be that I may obtain children by her. And Abram hearkened to the voice of Sarai." (Genesis 16:2). When Sarai was impatient and went ahead of God's plan, there were consequences to pay. Disobedience brought Ishmael, the Arab nation, and Isaac, the nation of Israel, to war. To this very day the two nations are fighting over their territories.

The time came when I made arrangements to move to another state. Whose voice was I hearing? Was it God's, my voice, or the voice of the enemy? God allowed it to happen. God allowed me and my family to take a journey through the wilderness and through the desert.

While my wife was on a missionary trip in London, England, my son and I traveled to Wisconsin to visit friends and look into the possibility of moving there. During our stay there, I found a job, an apartment, a church, and a school. I even found a job for Laura at the school our son would be attending, at their day-care center.

I called Laura one evening while she was on the mission trip and said, "How would you like to move to Wisconsin?" She commented, "Are you sure this is in God's plan?" I answered, "Of course I'm sure." I ended up bringing my family to a new part of the country that we were unfamiliar with. The main reason we were considering the move was because a friend and pastor from years ago was going to mentor me in preparation for ministry.

During our trip back home to New England, my son and I encountered fires burning along the interstate highway and in the adjacent woods. When we reached a toll booth, I asked the attendant about the fires. He advised us that the Indians were not happy at the reservation and were rioting due to a new tax law that was passed. The Indians were using old tires, and to set them ablaze, they were using gasoline. My son was excited to see the fires. The highway workers used loaders to remove the burning tires from the highway. It was 2:00 A.M., and I was concerned for our safety. I pulled into a gas station and spent time in prayer. I thanked God for His protection and asked for a continued hedge of protection around us, my wife, and the ministry team in Europe.

When we arrived home from our trip, my wife had everything packed and ready to load onto a rental truck. We were all excited to explore the new territories we had planned. The next week we picked up the rental truck and trailer, and loaded up all our belongings. On our day of departure, we awoke early. We had loaded our Jeep on the trailer the night before, so Laura was going to have to follow me in her car.

After traveling a number of hours, my wife and I got separated in Chattanooga, Tennessee, because of a "No Trucks Allowed" sign on the highway. My wife couldn't negotiate the exit in time because of the busy traffic.

With no contingency plans should this situation take place, we were at the mercy of each other's speculations. I had our son, Tommy, with me and proceeded to get back on the highway to search for my wife. I drove up a ramp only to find out the tunnel up ahead did have the necessary clearance but I was headed in the wrong direction. Laura, on the other hand, was driving around the city streets. I called my parents and alerted them, telling them if they heard from Laura to get her location and tell her to stay put and I would be calling back to check on her.

I returned to the truck and started heading toward the highway when I recognized my wife's car on the side of the road. She was in the car praying and crying. I had prayed earlier and asked God to reunite us. God's hand brought us back together. Praise

Jesus! That was enough excitement for one day, so we decided to stop and stay overnight as soon we found lodging.

It took another hour to find a motel, and by then we were physically and emotionally exhausted. After finally getting some sleep, we awoke, had breakfast, and got back into our driving routine. This time we made sure we weren't going to get separated.

The weather was unbearable as far as driving was concerned. It was so foggy that at times we couldn't even see the road or the fronts of our vehicles. Finally after driving for three days, we reached our destination at 12:00 A.M.

Upon arriving at the apartment, I was excited to show my wife our new home. When Laura took one look at our new apartment, her countenance dropped and she started crying. We had moved from an apartment in the East, which we only lived in for a short period of time. But before that apartment, we had lived in an absolutely lovely condominium. My wife at this point was not a happy woman. I thought, "After all, how bad could it be?" It was clean, close to town, offered a pool and tennis courts, all at an affordable price.

The next day we moved in, signed the final rental agreement documents, and returned our rental truck. We visited our friends and spent time in fellowship with them. They took us to visit our new church, school, and day-care center, all located within the same building. We all got acquainted with our new pastor and his family, and Laura's new supervisor. Tommy met his new teacher. She was a kind and gentle person. The people we met were a blessing. Everyone was so helpful.

We returned to our new home and settled in. In a few days I was going to be starting work on a large farm. I was anticipating that everything would go according to plan. I found out quickly that trusting someone isn't always easy.

My new boss was a lot different from my former boss on the farm back East. I was used to an honest person. When the man said you're hired to do various types of work, he meant it. My new boss had hidden intentions. He would say one thing but mean another. I had been subjected to many filthy jobs in the past, but that wasn't the problem. The problem, despite his dishonesty, was that he needed to give me every dirty job he could. I think he was totally heartless when it came to delegating duties. I couldn't even suggest a part that was needed to repair a machine. He ignored me like I didn't even exist. I didn't need to travel hundreds of miles to do someone's dirty work. I thought afterwards, "Why hadn't this prominent farmer hired someone from his own state."

I'll never forget one windy day when I was out spraying crops. The over-spray was coming into the cab. The air conditioning wasn't working and the floorboard where the clutch and brake pedals were was stuffed with dirty rags. I called the owner on the two-way radio and advised him I was getting sick from the over-spray. His response was, "Finish up the day and then you'll be all set." I explained again that it was very windy and I was getting sick. He asked me again to complete the work. I told him I would be returning to the farm shortly. I couldn't work under those conditions.

The other interesting point about the sprayer was that it had air brakes, which was great. The only problem was they leaked, and the unit didn't have an emergency brake, which meant if the engine stalled and you were in traffic on an incline, you would soon find out that the brakes did not work. One day after I had been operating the sprayer for a couple of weeks, my boss finally decided to share this interesting safety point with me.

I finally decided to quit the job. I couldn't believe how surprised he was when I told him things were not working out as planned. I couldn't understand why he originally made the job appear to be different than it really was. I had been misinformed about my job responsibilities. I was happy to move on to seek another job opportunity.

The next job I had was for a construction company, working as a heavy-equipment operator. I enjoyed the job operating the heavy construction equipment. Basically there were no hidden agendas and the work was pretty straightforward. The job lasted for a few months, and because I was not interested in snow removal, I was given a layoff slip.

While I was unemployed, I took advantage of spending some quality time with my wife and son. I attended the field trips that were offered at Tommy's school, visiting many area parks, zoos, and various interesting attractions. I loved spending time with my family.

My friend who had offered to mentor me didn't make the least attempt to disciple me. When I asked him if he was free to conduct an evening service with me, he told me, "Don't get too busy now." He discouraged me when it came to moving out in ministry.

I was still blessed because my new pastor offered me the opportunity to preach at a nursing home. I was excited and accepted his offer.

My wife and I had attended the weekly nursing home services for a while, and finally it was my week to preach. Our music ministry team participated in the opening of the service, and we all sang songs of praises and thanksgiving to our Lord Jesus Christ and Savior. After a number of songs, we finished singing. The room was filled with the presence of God.

This was my first time preaching and my heart started pounding. I opened the service with prayer and shared a message on God's love for each and every one of us. The focus of my message is found in the Gospel of John: "For God so loved the world, that He gave his only begotten Son, that whosoever believeth in him should not perish, but have everlasting life" (John 3:16). I spoke about Jesus Christ's unconditional love for each one of us. He paid the ultimate price for our redemption. "For ye are bought with a price: therefore glorify God in your body, and in your spirit, which are God's" (1Corinthians 6:20). I explained that Jesus suffered for each of us. "But He was wounded for our transgressions, He was bruised for our iniquities: the chastisement of our peace was upon Him; and with His stripes we are healed" (Isaiah 53:5). I shared about our Lord's walk on earth. His walk was a walk of love. He healed many, delivered many, and led a sinless life. He was perfect, yet He took the nails and the cross for each one of us. What a wonderful God we serve! I ended in prayer and asked if anyone would like to receive Jesus Christ as their personal Savior.

As time progressed, our plans weren't working out as expected. Actually, what should I have expected, going ahead of God, and traveling hundreds of miles to a new state, new surroundings, new career, and all? My wife was growing weary of her work at the day-care center also. What started out as an adventure was turning into drudgery.

At least there were positive attributes. Our family was healthy, our son was enrolled in a Christian school, his teacher loved Jesus and was a fond educator and person, and we attended a Christian church. Also, we loved Jesus and we had many supportive Christian friends. Our love for each other increased, and unlike my workaholic days, which stole from my family life, we were spending more quality family time together.

I remember receiving a word from the Lord through a prophet during a special service back East. He said: "All you do is work, work, work. Stop working so much and spend time with thy wife." The word I received was exactly on target, on time and to the point. God's timing is always perfect. I learned through the years that nothing can take the place of quality time with my wife and son.

The lesson I have learned was to focus on the needs of my family by sharing the word, praying, attending church services, and by doing things together. I found out I needed to be available to tend to their needs. I believe God used this time in the wilderness with my family to deepen the roots of love in our lives together. We became more dependent upon God and each other. We had a cross to bear, and in bearing our cross, we were more able to crucify our flesh. "There is therefore now no condemnation to them which are in Christ Jesus, who walk not after the flesh, but after the Spirit" (Romans 8:1).

Part 2

Though we spent time in the wilderness, now it was time to spend time in the desert. We prayed and thought about traveling down south but didn't wait for a sign from the Lord. "And the peace of God, which passeth all understanding, shall keep your hearts and minds through Christ Jesus" (Philippians 4:7). My wife and I had generated our own peace, which wasn't the proper thing to do. We thought it would be better living closer to my parents. Our other ambition was to be closer to another ministry in the area. I headed for the warm climate of Florida and my parents met me at the airport. They had moved to Florida eighteen years before. We all had gone through many learning experiences as a family, and we were very close. I missed and loved them dearly. My intention was to visit them, look for employment, and a place to live. After a few days we headed for Orlando. My parents and I ended up staying at a dear friend's home in the area. She always made us feel part of her family. While my parents and friend visited, I spent time searching the newspaper and finally made a contact. A local electrical contractor was looking for an electrician, and he set up an appointment with me for an interview. After so many years of owning and operating an electrical contracting business, it was a humbling experience. Following the interview I was offered the position. I told the supervisor I would let him know my decision soon. I thought about the position and then called Laura in Wisconsin to ask her and to pray with her about it. She was so excited about possibly leaving the cold and relocating to a more amenable climate. I told her I would wait to find an apartment that she would definitely like before I called the supervisor and accepted the job.

I spent the next day looking at many different apartments and condominiums and finally found what seemed to be a nice one. The unit was reasonably priced, cozy, and would be completely cleaned, new carpeting installed in the living room, and freshly painted. The amenities included a pool, sauna, hot tub, tennis courts, and use of the meeting room. I talked with the rental agent concerning my past credit history, and because of my poor credit rating, a higher deposit than normal was going to be required. She reassured me it shouldn't be a problem.

I called Laura and shared the information with her. She was getting more and more excited. Our son was happy at the thought of being able to swim on a routine basis, wear shorts, and play in the sand. My wife and I again prayed and brought the opportunity to God for His direction. We didn't receive an answer from the Lord because we didn't wait and listen for His answer. "But they that wait upon the Lord shall renew their strength; they shall mount up with wings as eagles; they shall run, and not be weary; and they shall walk, and not faint" (Isaiah 40:31). My wife and I decided to make Florida our new home. So, I called my new supervisor and he set a date for me to report to work.

My dad has a big heart and he offered to assist us financially, even though each time we moved we were getting further and further in debt. Two days later, I returned to Wisconsin and started to make preparations to move to Florida. I planned to haul our belongings to Florida and store them for two weeks. Everything went according to plan; we picked up the rental truck, loaded it up, and said good-bye to our friends.

The next day early in the morning we headed for sunny Florida. We all drove in the rental truck together on this trip because we had sold our Jeep and were hauling our car on a trailer. We spent two nights at motels on the way to Florida and loved the trip together. When we arrived in Florida, we unloaded the truck together at the storage unit and returned the vehicle. My parents met us and we enjoyed having dinner and spending time together. Laura and Tommy drove back home with my parents the next day. Now I wouldn't be seeing them until the weekend. I wasn't used to being away from them and they were deeply missed. I started my new electrical job the next day. I went to work not knowing what to expect. I had only a few jobs working for other employers after being self-employed for nineteen years. Actually I had forgotten what it was like to have to report directly to a supervisor. It was a humbling experience to take directions from men that were half my age. Some of the work that I was directed to do just wasn't practical, but I learned to make the best of the situation. "Humble yourselves therefore under the mighty hand of God, that he may exalt you in due time" (1 Peter 5:6).

After working a week with my new employer, the supervisor was pleased with my performance, which gave me a sense of encouragement. I was assigned to a crew who was wiring a new church and was pleased to be part of the project. As soon as I was released from work on Friday afternoons, I immediately headed for my parents' home in southern Florida. I couldn't wait to see my wife, son, mom, and dad. I loved the time we spent together now on the weekends.

When I was self-employed, my life was not my own. I was very dedicated to my clients and they were very demanding, which took up hours and hours of my time and energies. I should have stopped to consider: Would God have approved of my lengthy daily activities that took away from my family life? I already knew the answer, and it was a positive no!

As a child of Christ, I really needed to turn my focus to God and praise Him for everything He was doing in my family's life.

On Sunday, Laura, Tommy, and I attended church together. Each moment we spent together was a blessing from God. We all gathered at my parents' house and enjoyed a delicious meal and fellowship together. After dinner we visited for a while, then I had to pack up to prepare for my work week.

Finally after traveling back and forth a few weeks, our apartment was ready. I hired a local trucker to haul our belongings to our new home. The man from the trucking company quoted me a reasonable price, considering the amount of furniture and other belongings we had to move. I met him at our storage area and loaded up his truck. We arranged to meet the following day at our new apartment. We unloaded all the furniture and various boxes and he departed. Now it was time for me to arrange the furniture and unpack the many boxes. It took a couple of days to get things pretty much in place. I anticipated where my wife would like the furniture and did my best to place it accordingly.

The next day my family would be coming home, and we'd be together once again. My parents were driving up with Laura and Tommy, and we were going to have dinner together. They arrived. At last we were reunited once again. When Laura and Tommy entered our new home, they were quite pleased with how everything looked, which made me happy.

Shortly after their arrival, I felt the need to share about our uninvited guests. Our apartment was infested with cockroaches–they were in the kitchen and in the closet where I stored the boxes that weren't unpacked. My wife got upset and it ended up being one of the most disgusting experiences of our lives. Every box in our closet was infested with roaches. All the boxes had to be thrown out and our new apartment had to be fumigated to rid it of the roaches. We never actually got over the roach problem.

The next major apartment-related event came to light when it rained. The water seeped through the walls in our bedroom and around the window casings in both our bedroom and living room. We called the maintenance staff and requested them to make the necessary repairs, which they tried to do, but the leaks never stopped. Many of our personal items were absorbing the moisture, and we had to start throwing them away. Even the new carpets smelled of mildew. Despite the living conditions, we tried to make light of it. We enjoyed the sunshine and warmth of the climate. To help defray expenses, my wife decided to get a job in the bakery across the street at a major grocery store.

As time marched on, we were getting deeper and deeper into debt. I was promised a raise, which never materialized, and we contemplated returning back East. With everything thing else going on in our lives, now we had to brace ourselves for a major emergency.

An emergency weather advisory was issued on television and radio of a tornado watch for the county we were living in. I really didn't take the warning seriously, but my wife did. She kept her eyes glued to the television and brought me the updated advisories.

That evening, my wife noticed the unusual sunset. The colors of the sky were purple, red, yellow, and green. Though I didn't think anything was going to happen, we still took the necessary precautions. My wife was watching the updates and they announced on television there were over ten sightings of tornadoes in the area. Laura woke me up and told me that we were possibly in danger and that the latest news report advised all residents to take cover. The next thing we did was to take all our pillows and cushions and bring them into the main bathroom. We set up a bed in the tub for our son and he fell asleep. Next I placed a mattress against the bathroom door. Laura started reading the Word and I prayed, as the winds, heavy rain, thunder and lightning continued to rage.

There were four to five tornado touchdowns, and they were category three or four. The tornados passed around us and leveled areas within ten to twenty minutes of our home. Whole communities were completely destroyed. We ended up staying in the bathroom for a few hours until the storm receded. Needless to say, we were shocked to hear, see, and read about the massive destruction in the area. We heard of people being swept away by the storm.

One miracle we heard about was a story concerning a baby being swept away: someone found the baby lying on a mattress in a tree, in good health. We thanked God for being our shield and our strength in time of need. "The Lord is my strength and my shield; my heart trusted in him, and I am helped: therefore my heart greatly rejoiced; and with my song will I praise him" (Psalm 28:7). After this episode, it was easier to make the decision to move back East.

I decided to call a business acquaintance back home to see if we could work out a plan. He answered the phone and was enthusiastic about talking with me. We chatted for a while concerning what was going on in our lives and about how our families were doing. We hadn't talked for three years and pretty much picked up where we left off. He advised me he had some ongoing projects that needed electrical wiring.

I decided to fly back East to meet with him to negotiate a contract. He even arranged to leave a vehicle at the airport for me. The topic covered at our meeting was full-time employment working in the electrical division of his company. The benefits included medical insurance, a company vehicle, vacation, holiday pay, and an advance in pay to help us with our relocation costs. He also signed a one-year contract with me and agreed to the salary which I requested. I spent some time traveling with him to various projects and appreciated his openness to hire me.

This opportunity was a huge blessing. I discussed the position and offer with Laura that evening and prayed about it. We both realized the need to return home.

It was now time to come back from our trip through the desert. God not only allowed us to go forward and live a dream, but he also protected us all the way through it.

It was time to go through the routine again: rent a truck, load it, say good-bye to our friends, and start the journey home. We were all excited again even though this time we were driving back to our home state. Laura was especially happy because we were going to move in with her mother. We spent three nights in motels and arrived back East.

When we moved in with my mother-in-law, we also were going to be living with Laura's sister, a brother-in-law, and two children. It proved to be a test in patience for all of us. To be honest it was almost impossible. Basically we invaded their territory. Laura started to look into a condominium, and bless her heart, found a beautiful home for us to live in. The owner had other people looking at the unit but told us she wanted to lease the unit to us even before she completed the credit check. God is so faithful. "Behold I will do a new thing; now it shall spring forth; shall ye not know it? I will even make a way in the wilderness, and rivers in the desert" (Isaiah 43:19).

Chapter 26

Prompting of
the Holy Spirit

It was a clear sunny day, midsummer, and I was traveling through Middleboro, Massachusetts on the interstate when I was prompted by the Holy Spirit to pray in tongues. "For he that speaketh in an unknown tongue speaketh not unto men, but unto God" (1Corinthians 14:2). Immediately I started praying and continued to pray for fifteen minutes. I noticed large chunks of truck tire rubber in the roadway. As I avoided the obstacles, the traffic started slowing down. Up ahead a car had rolled over and landed on the driver's side of the vehicle. I pulled up to a safe spot ahead of the accident scene and parked.

I called 911 on my cellular phone and reported the accident to the state police dispatcher. I jumped out of the truck next and went over to check on the driver, but there was no driver to be found. Next I checked for gasoline leaks and made sure the ignition was turned off. To my amazement, there were no leaks of any type.

I noticed a car on the shoulder of the road and saw a man waving to me. He shouted to me and said the driver of the car was with him. Crossing the traffic, I finally reached him and the driver who was sitting in his car. The man told me he'd arrived at the scene just minutes before me. The driver was a young girl in her teens sitting in his car resting, without a scratch but subdued from the trauma she had just experienced. I asked her if I could pray for her. As we prayed she acknowledged that Jesus had saved her life today and we thanked Him. We asked for His strength and peace upon her life. I asked her if she had a relationship with Jesus and she said, "Yes, and my family does too." I thanked Jesus again for saving her life and we talked about how much Jesus loves her. I gave her a booklet to read about Jesus.

Evidently, when she swerved to try to avoid the chunks of rubber in the road she lost control of the car and then it flipped and landed on its side. The car was only slightly damaged, but it was a convertible, which could have been disastrous. The only advantage was the fact she escaped from the car without difficulty because she released the roof latch to get free.

The police arrived shortly after we prayed together, and the ambulance followed. I told her she would be in good hands now, and it was time for me to leave.

I was so blessed to have been able to intercede on her behalf when the Holy Spirit prompted me to do so. I was in tears when I left the accident scene and felt so touched by God to have witnessed His miracle, which was a true expression of His character of love and compassion. This young girl was shielded, protected, and safe from even the slightest of injuries. "But thou, O Lord, art a shield for me; my glory, and the lifter up of mine head" (Psalm 3:3).

Chapter 27

Waiting on the Lord

After working for a communications company for four months, I was dismissed from work because of the company's financial problems, which led to the closing of the business. A client, whom I knew well, worked in an office locally, so I called the manager and set up an appointment with him. We talked and discussed my situation, and I filed an application for employment with him. He in turn forwarded my application and resume to the appropriate person. I called one week later and was given a telephone interview. Within two weeks, I was offered a position as a project manager in New York City or Washington, DC.

My family was concerned about our location and really wanted and needed to be in God's will. Laura and I should have learned from our previous experience not to jump in and make plans ahead of God. Laura and I planned a trip with our son Tommy to Washington, DC so we could check out the area and I could speak with the man who would be my potential supervisor. The day before we were to leave for our trip, the director called and offered me a position locally. I told him I had already planned a trip with my family to Washington, DC to check out the area and give us time to spend together. He responded by saying: "Okay, keep me informed of your decision."

We headed for Washington, DC and were all happy to be together. We stayed just outside DC in a comfortable motel. I drove into the city the next day and met with the supervisor. I enjoyed my conversation with him and he gave me a tour of the facility. I told him I'd be talking with his boss in a week about my decision.

When I arrived at the motel, my wife asked me about the particulars regarding my meeting. I told her everything went fine, but we needed to seek God's face for an answer.

The job locally would have been the easiest option to accept. During the week of our stay in the Washington, DC area, Laura had the opportunity to visit a friend, and my son and I were able to visit the Smithsonian Institute. While we were in the area, we checked out schools for Tommy. We also looked at apartments and condos and found a lovely home just right across the street from a school where our son could attend.

We spent a lot of time and effort looking for a place to live and wanted to secure a home in the area in the event we indeed were going to relocate. So we placed a deposit on our potential new home. What we really needed to do was to wait on God for our answer and not go any further with unnecessary arrangements. "Wait on the Lord: be of good courage, and he shall strengthen thine heart: wait, I say, on the Lord" (Psalm 27:14).

We continued to ask God for His direction, but we were too anxious. "Be anxious for nothing; but in everything by prayer and supplication with thanksgiving let your requests be made known unto God" (Philippians 4:6). Prayer is the key to receiving an answer from God. Sometimes it's hard to admit when I'm wrong, but sharing openly gives the devil no leverage regarding the truth. The truth has always caused a higher degree of healing and comfort for me, though initially I thought differently.

When we arrived home from our trip, I was tense. Laura asked if we could pray together and I told her, "Later." That selfish mistake could have cost the lives of my mother-in-law, wife, and son. There have been times when I asked Laura to come together and pray, and she wouldn't agree. After her reluctance to pray, she has gotten into two accidents. If there is any blame to be given regarding the accident when we returned from Washington, DC, I am totally responsible because I hadn't taken the time to pray.

Laura and Tommy left our home to run an errand with my mother-in-law. They were involved in a motor vehicle accident not even a mile away from our house. My wife was sitting in the passenger seat, and even though the car was going no faster than a few miles per hour upon impact, she was blasted in the face by the car's air bag, which left her unconscious and suffering with extreme burns on her face and a broken nose. She also suffered injuries to her neck. Laura's mom sustained a laceration on her arm from her air bag, and our son couldn't breathe too well because of the smoke from the air bags exploding. He thought the engine exploded and ended up getting out of the car on the unsafe side of the road because the child safety lock was set on the rear door. He exited into the oncoming traffic alone and walked around the car to a safe place beyond the curb. Thank God he was safe.

An ambulance happened to be driving by and stopped at the accident scene. Laura was strapped on a backboard and taken to the hospital. My sister- in-law drove to our house shortly after the accident and told me my wife was being taken to the hospital. When I arrived at the hospital, I couldn't believe the poor condition my wife was in. She looked like she had been in a high-speed collision. She was semiconscious now, and as I started to pray I knew God had spared her life.

Later on she asked how Tommy was, and I told her fine. He too was spared by the hand of God. Laura's mom was also doing okay. We were so blessed to have everyone still alive and not disabled.

God didn't orchestrate the accident, but He did let it happen. My wife and I neglected coming together and searching out God's will before we made any plans concerning our move. We started making plans to move with our agenda in mind, not with God's in mind. This time God was not going to allow us to get ahead of Him. I am very thankful to God for His mercy and His grace in protecting my family from death or becoming severely disabled. "He brought me up also out of a horrible pit, out of the miry clay, and set my feet upon a rock, and established my goings" (Psalm 40:2).

Laura is still suffering from neck pain, and we believe God is in the process of healing her. "He sent his word, and healed them, and delivered them from their destructions" (Psalm 107:20). My Jesus is so faithful!

Chapter 28

Dad's Healing

In December of 2001, my mom called me to inform me that my dad was in the hospital in Florida. His doctor was unable to successfully perform a procedure that my father desperately needed due to blockages in his heart. The problem was that his network of veins and arteries crossed back and forth throughout his body. I might add that this particular doctor has completed over thirty-five thousand procedures. My mom was very upset, and after talking a little while, we prayed together and I told her I would call Dad and pray for him as soon as we got off the phone. I called him immediately and prayed for him. I was believing God was going to intercede on behalf of my father and we would all see His glory at work. "Who forgiveth all thine iniquities; who healeth all thy diseases" (Psalm 103:3).

I knew in my heart I needed to leave for Florida soon to give my parents support. I called my brother and talked with him for a while and asked him if he could help me with the finances for my trip to Florida. My trip would enable me to pray with my mom and dad and to give my mother some encouragement. I told my brother I wanted to leave immediately, and he agreed to assist me. When I called him back we arranged to meet at the airport, and I filled him in with all the details. I was actually able to book a flight that was departing in the morning. Thank you Jesus!

I awakened early in the morning to spend time in prayer and this was also the day I completed my seven-day fast. I asked God to see my dad through this procedure. I asked God to direct the physician through the hand of Jesus as if He were performing the procedure Himself and also asked Him to direct the nurses and hospital staff. "Ask and it shall be given you; seek, and you shall find; knock, and it shall be opened unto you" (Matthew 7:7).

I was on fire in prayer as I believed and trusted in God for my father's miracle. I also asked God to delay my father's procedure until I was able to reach his bedside because I wanted to ask my parents to recommit their lives to their Lord and Savior Jesus Christ. "And all things, whatsoever ye shall ask in prayer, believing, ye shall receive" (Matthew 21:22). I wanted God to allow me to reach my father in time to pray and lay hands on him to heal him in the name of Jesus. "They shall lay hands on the sick and they shall recover" (Mark 16:18b). I continued to press in and thanked God for hearing my prayers.

It was now time to prepare myself for my trip. My flight to visit my dad and mom was leaving in just a few hours. My ride arrived at my house early in the morning and I said good-bye to Laura and Tommy and told them I would miss them dearly. Though I would have loved their company, now wasn't the time for them to come along. My friend left me at the airport and I hurried to get through all the preflight procedures and board the plane. I realized it wouldn't be very long before I would be with my parents. Once I got settled in and the airplane leveled off at our flying altitude, I fell asleep. The Holy Spirit spoke to me and said: "You will be a blessing to your family." The last words were: "How do you make bread"? I understood the part about a blessing, even though I didn't know to what extent the blessing would be, and I wasn't about to question God regarding a blessing. But Lord, is that you asking me how to make bread. But I realized the scripture that states, "For my thoughts are not your thoughts, neither are your ways my ways, saith the Lord" (Isaiah 55:8). I decided to answer the question the best I could and put it on the shelf for a later discussion with the Lord.

My flight arrived on time and without the slightest problem. Praise God! I got off the plane, picked up my luggage, and headed for the limousine service for the transportation I needed to get to the hospital. I talked to the agent and he advised me of the various rate charges. He said, "If you wait a little longer the rate will be cheaper, but if you're in a hurry you might want the ride that is more expensive." I thought, *Lord I need to get to my dad quickly but I needed to be wise, I already borrowed money from my brother, what shall I do?* I didn't receive a peace about trying to get there any quicker, so I chose the less expensive transportation.

I waited and waited and now started to wonder if I was really doing the right thing. I asked God again, *Am I doing the right thing by waiting?* Finally my ride showed up and I got in the car and we left the airport. The ride to the hospital was going to take about an hour.

As we were traveling, I wondered if my dad would still be in his hospital room when I arrived, and wondered if his procedure was delayed. I didn't really think I needed to know what the man sitting next to me did for a living but I felt a nudge from the Lord to ask. I asked, "What do you do for work?" He answered me, "I work at a food processing plant." I said, "What products do you make?" He responded, "We make different types of bread." I chuckled to myself and thought, *Holy Spirit, you certainly have a sense of humor.* I knew the moment this man said "bread" that I was in the right place at the right time and that God was responding to my prayers.

When I arrived at the hospital, I couldn't find the elevators at first because of the construction work taking place. Once I was in the elevator, a volunteer said, "How are you today?" I said that I was good, but if I knew how my father was, I'd be even better. She said, "Is he having a procedure done today"? I said yes. When I did, she told me that my father was still in his room waiting to be brought into the operating room. At that point I said, "Thank you, God; praise you Jesus!" I practically ran when I got off the elevator.

When I reached Dad's room, I was so happy to see both of my parents, I hugged and kissed my mom and dad, and by then I was in tears. We visited for a moment and then I said to them that I needed to pray for both of them. I reached in my luggage and pulled out my dispenser of anointing oil. I anointed them with oil and proceeded to pray for them. I prayed for their inner strength, peace and complete healing. I discussed these Scripture verses with them: "That if thou shalt confess with thy mouth the Lord Jesus, and shalt believe in thine heart that God hath raised him from the dead, thou shalt be saved" (Romans 10:9). And "FOR WHOSOVER SHALL CALL UPON THE NAME OF THE LORD SHALL BE SAVED" (Romans 10:13).

The time we shared and prayed together was in the presence of the Lord and was so powerful. My dad's nurse came in and informed us that his procedure wouldn't be scheduled until tomorrow now, which was a relief to me–I could spend more time in prayer. I visited with my mom and dad for the rest of the day. Early in the evening, it was time to let my dad get some rest. We planned on returning first thing in the morning. My mom and I left and headed to their lovely home. When we arrived, I visited with her for a while and then spent time in prayer. I thanked God for everything he was doing in their lives and reflected on my prayer list.

I called home to talk with Laura and share God's blessings with her, and also talked with Tommy and told both of them I missed and loved them very much. It was now time to call it a day–the whole day was great in the Lord, Praise you, Jesus! Early in the morning I got up and spent time in prayer, got ready, and headed for the hospital with my mom.

When we arrived, my dad was up and waiting to be told by his doctor when his operation was scheduled. I was waiting on the Lord, and I believed He was going to move. I had expectations of a powerful move of God through faith. "With men this is impossible; but with God all things are possible" (Matthew 19:26). My dad was going to be the last patient of the day, which the doctor planned so he could spend more time with my father. The doctor was a blessing, and I appreciated his concern for my dad and his willingness to persevere. He was an expert in his field.

Throughout the day I had the opportunity to witness in the hospital about Jesus. I was able to talk with patients, families, and staff members. I remember a man who didn't believe me about Jesus. He told me he'd watched ministers on television and said the healings were fake and that they weren't real and it was a show.

I've worked at crusades as a usher, and I have seen the miracles firsthand, and told him he shouldn't be concentrating on what the people were doing; people are only willing vessels of God. I asked him if he wanted to be healed, forgiven, and given God's greatest miracle, which is eternal life. His question was, "Who's going to do it, you?" I told him again, no, God is able and willing. I am here to help you by bringing Christ to you. I'm talking to you about my Master, my Savior, my Jesus, and my Lord. I continued to ask him if he'd like to receive Jesus Christ. He said, "No." His next question was, "Could my heart be healed?" I said to him, "Yes, and please realize that God is the healer. Receiving Jesus as your Savior will ensure that you will have eternal life if you commit yourself to God sincerely in your heart and recite the sinner's prayer."

Then the man started getting upset, even though I was being honest with him. I tried to direct him to Christ and told him God was able to change his life. I was so on fire and excited, talking about what Christ can do, will do, and is ready to do for him that nothing fazed me concerning his insults. God made it very clear to me when He spoke to me and said: "Some people are not ready to receive me." I told him I needed to get back to my father and reassured him that I would continue to pray for him.

When I got back to my father's room, I learned that he was scheduled for 6:00 P.M. My mom and I were both in the hospital room when my father was taken to the procedure room. I knew God was going to move. I was expecting a positive report from the nurse. My mom and I prayed together and waited together for about two hours. The nurse finally came out and said, "The doctor has completed the procedure." I said, "Yes, yes." Then she said, "The procedure was a success." My immediate answer was, "Praise God!" Next I meditated, focusing on the Lord, giving Him thanks and praise for being so faithful.

Then the nurse said, "Would you like to see him?" We said, "Definitely." When my mom and I walked in to see my dad, he was still connected to all the monitors and other equipment. I asked Dad how he was doing and he said, "Fine." We were so pleased to see that the procedure was completed. The doctor showed my mom and me on the monitor why the procedure was so difficult. I told the doctor, "Thank God," and that we were praying for him. The doctor thanked us for praying for him.

After spending a few more minutes with my dad, I hurried out to call my wife and give her the good news. She was so happy and relieved. Shortly after we left the room, my dad was taken back to his room. When I walked in, he said, "Son, you have just experienced a miracle." I said to him, "God is so faithful. He answers prayers–thank you, Lord!" We stayed for just a little while longer, then my mom and I left for home to make sure Dad would get his rest.

On our way back to my parent's house, my mom was so pleased and relieved about my dad's condition. Many people had been praying for his healing. "Again I say unto you, That if two of you shall agree on earth as touching any thing that they shall ask, it shall be done for them of my Father which is in heaven" (Matthew 18:19).

My dad was discharged from the hospital the next day, and he enjoyed being back in his home. I spent two more days with my parents, and we had a blessed time together. I was given a ride to the airport from a friend of my parents and was so excited to know I would be seeing my wife and son soon. My flight went well, and my family was waiting for me with open arms. I felt so blessed to see them when I arrived. "Blessed be the Lord, who daily loadeth us with benefits, even the God of our salvation" (Psalm 68:19).

Chapter 29

Listen, Pray, and Learn to Obey

For several years, the Lord had been showing me how powerful listening, praying, and obeying really is. The Holy Spirit has directed me to pray early in the morning for a number of years. In the past it has been a struggle, but over time I've learned to press in. I've always needed to do what God was leading me to do from my heart and I have learned that I should never question Him, just obey Him. However, some mornings I'd wake up to pray and fall right back asleep.

During my encounter with laziness, I was given a dream by the Lord that helped me to change my prayer habits. God showed me that I needed to be faithful because my requests to Him would not be answered without spending time with Him. "My voice shalt thou hear in the morning, O Lord; in the morning will I direct my prayer unto thee, and will look up" (Psalm 5:3). It was as if He was telling me I needed a breakthrough in my dedicated time with Him, which was absolutely true.

I always had the energy to work in the ambulance and fight fires, working all hours of the day and night, even when I was self-employed. But what happened to my energy level when it came to being obedient to God? The most difficult part of being thoughtless and lazy with God has been the fact that He has awakened me in my sleep to fellowship with Him, and I in turn have fallen right back asleep. I knew He longed to fellowship with me, and I felt disappointed in myself that I didn't follow through. Thank God, He is a God of mercy, grace, and forgiveness. He was showing me that continuing to work countless hours in the corporate world and neglecting Him could bring consequences upon me that were unnecessary. I was falling asleep because I was giving God my leftovers from my daily routine. What happened to my prayer life with God?

Over the years, God has been using me in intercessory prayer, and He was ensuring that I would be obedient to Him by getting my attention. I have repented because of my slacking-off period and have asked God for forgiveness. My prayer time now is a powerful, exciting, and a much-needed intimate time communicating with God. I look forward to my prayer time with the Holy Spirit, not only in the early morning but throughout the day. "Evening, and morning and at noon, will I pray, and cry aloud: and he shall hear my voice" (Psalm 55:17). A powerful scripture regarding the effectiveness of prayer is found in James 5:16: "Confess your faults one to another, and pray one for another, that ye may be healed. The effectual fervent prayer of a righteous man availeth much."

The seven key steps in my life where the Holy Spirit has made it perfectly clear that I need to focus, concentrate, and expend my energies to bring me closer to the Lord and to a place of intimacy with Jesus are listed below:

1. Prayer–Hearken unto the voice of my cry, my King, and my God; for unto thee will I pray (Psalm 5:2).
2. Fasting–Is not this the fast that I have chosen? to loose the bands of wickedness, to undo the heavy burdens, and let the oppressed go free, and that ye break every yoke? (Isaiah 58:6).
3. Praise–Let the people praise thee, O God; let all the people praise thee. Then shall the earth yield her increase; and God, even our own God, shall bless us (Psalm 67:5-6). So the spirit took me up, and brought me into the inner court; and, behold, the glory of the Lord filled the house (Ezekiel 43:5).
4. Reading the Word–For the word of God is quick, and powerful, and sharper than any twoedged sword, piercing even to the dividing asunder in soul and spirit, and of the joints and marrow, and is a discerner of the thoughts and intents of the heart (Hebrews 4:12).

5. Meditating and Studying the Word–But his delight is in the law of the Lord; and in his law doth he meditate day and night (Psalm 1:2). Study to show thyself approved unto God, a workman that needeth not to be ashamed, rightly dividing the word of truth (2 Timothy 2:15).
6. Fellowship–That which we have seen and heard declare we unto you, that ye also may have fellowship with us; and truly our fellowship is with the Father, and with his Son Jesus Christ (1 John 1:3).
7. Witness–But ye shall receive power, after that the Holy Ghost is come upon you: and ye shall be witnesses unto me both in Jerusalem, and in all Judaea, and in Samaria, and unto the uttermost part of the earth (Acts 1:8).

The steps you have read have also strengthened me and enabled me to prepare for spiritual warfare. Here are a few Scriptures that have helped me with my constant fight with the devil: "The thief cometh not, but for to steal, and to kill, and to destroy: I am come that they might have life, and that they might have it more abundantly" (John 10:10).

"Submit yourselves therefore to God. Resist the devil, and he will flee from you" (James 4:7).

The Lord has explicitly directed me to apply my armor daily: "Put on the whole armor of God, that ye may be able to stand against the wiles of the devil. For we wrestle not against flesh and blood, but against principalities, against powers, against the rulers of the darkness of this world, against spiritual wickedness in high places. Wherefore take unto you the whole armor of God, that ye may be able to withstand in the evil day, and having done all, to stand. Stand therefore, having your loins girt about with truth, and having on the breastplate of righteousness; And your feet shod with the preparation of the gospel of peace; Above all, taking the shield of faith, wherewith ye shall be able to quench all the fiery darts of the wicked. And take the helmet of salvation, and the sword of the Spirit, which is the word of God" (Ephesians 6:11-17).

Chapter 30

Ministry Experience

One day, while I was shopping for gifts at a Christian book store, I met one of the clerks. He caught my attention because he was helpful, friendly, humble, and open for discussion. We talked for a while about the Lord until he had to get back to his work.

When I brought the articles to the counter, he took care of me. We talked again and planned on getting together to fellowship. He told me he'd be going into the hospital for an operation, and I told him I'd keep him in prayer. I thought maybe I could help him out in some way.

Time passed and we'd talk and pray occasionally, but we never got together. In my spirit I knew God was in the midst of our relationship because I felt connected to him. Now I had to wait to see what God's plan really was.

Two years later, while I was getting ready to leave the same store, he drove in. We were blessed to see each other. After we talked for a while, he asked me if I'd like to attend a prayer breakfast sponsored by Faith Outreach Ministries, scheduled for the next day in Springfield, Massachusetts. I was delighted to be invited. I had my son Tommy with me and he told me Tommy was welcome also. I told him I would definitely try to make it. He also told me he'd like to call on me to share my testimony. I responded by saying, "What testimony?" He said, "Oh, I'm sure you have one."

My mind started working overtime. I thought back to when I suffered my severe depression when I was sixteen. I thought no, I'm not sharing that with anyone. Little did I know what God had planned and what was actually going to transpire. I told my friend

I'd be praying about which testimony I'd share, said good-bye and left the store. I drove home with Tommy and then called someone to watch him during the morning prayer breakfast. I thought he'd enjoy playing on a Saturday instead of coming along.

When I reached the restaurant, I walked in and realized I was the only white man in a black man's gathering. God was teaching me a lesson as I came in the door, and there were more lessons to come. Years and years ago I was a bit prejudiced, but God was teaching me that the color of one's skin is not the issue of His creation of mankind to be concerned about. It is one's heart that should be my concern. In other words, I should be seeking the best for people by praying that their hearts would turn to God.

The people at the breakfast couldn't have been any nicer, any more accommodating, or any more genuine. I looked around and said to the Lord, "God, you are awesome for bringing me here to fellowship with your people. Thank you, Lord." I was greeted by my friend who was the only person I knew in the restaurant. He asked me to sit with him at his table with other brothers and sisters in Christ. I talked with the people at the table and they made me feel right at home. Shortly after I sat down, my friend came over to me and said, "Are you ready to give your testimony?" My answer was, "Which one?" His response was, "Whatever one you have is the one. You must have one to share, don't you?" I was still searching my heart and didn't want to give in to myself because the one I thought of was the most hurtful to share, and the one which hurt the most in my life.

After praying about it again, I received a peace in preparing myself to share the testimony that brought me closer to death than I could ever imagine or dream of. I turned myself over to Jesus and said, "Lord I don't know how to share this experience. Please show me the way and give me the words." "For it is not ye that speak, but the Spirit of your Father which speaketh in you" (Matthew 10:20).

The meeting started with prayer and a blessing of the food. Various speakers and singers were called up throughout the breakfast, one after another. There were powerful testimonies, and powerful songs of intimate praises to the Lord. I experienced people who were on fire for Jesus Christ. The presence of the Holy Spirit was so powerful and awesome. The main speaker was now called up, and she preached a powerful word. She too was on fire for Jesus, and she was flowing in the rivers of living water. "If any man thirst, let him come unto me, and drink. He that believeth on me, as the scripture hath said, out of his belly shall flow rivers of living water" (John 7:37-38). Glory to God, the fire of the Holy Sprit was burning in the hearts of his people.

By this time I was ignited by the fire and knew I was going to be called on very soon. My heart started pounding, and I could almost count the beats. I was called next. At first I was nervous, then the Holy Spirit took over as I gave my testimony concerning my depression years ago, which I shared in chapter ten. This was the first time I had ever shared this testimony. "They overcame him by the blood of the Lamb, and by the word of their testimony" (Revelation 12:11a).

As I walked away from the podium I was so enriched in Christ. I felt my heart was so much lighter, having released a heavy burden. I had a new level of confidence in Christ.

Because I came forward and opened up and shared my failures and sufferings, it enabled people to see how sovereign God really is. God was the only reason I was able to live through my depression. There is no doubt about it. All through my childhood I was taught to be a very private person and to never openly share anything personal with anybody. The only problem with that attitude is that God shares everything with us, especially in His written and spoken word. Why is it I couldn't share my sufferings with other people? Because I was placed in bondage. The burden I held onto for twenty-two years was now released. No, I didn't have to be ashamed of my near-death experience or answer to anyone about how I got myself into the situation. I was free to share my horrifying experience openly. After all, everything about our Lord is written in the Bible, and He is our mighty God.

Why couldn't I be an open book also? I was a captive who was set free. God wants every one of his people to be set free. When the truth is revealed, Satan can't antagonize us with what's hidden anymore, which he will try to do one way or another. "And ye shall know the truth, and the truth shall make you free" (John 8:32). When we come forth under the light, God brings upon us inner healing through His truth. "But if we walk in the light, as he is in the light, we have fellowship one with another, and the blood of Jesus Christ his Son cleanseth us from all sin" (1John 1:7).

Many people present at the breakfast told me they enjoyed my powerful testimony. I thanked them for their encouragement. One pastor came up to me and gave me his card and said, "Maybe you'll like to share your testimony on Christian radio, please give me a call." Another pastor asked me to share my testimony with his youth group. My friend who invited me to the breakfast asked me to be part of their outreach ministry group a few weeks later. He also told me that the group ministered at the prisons. I was delighted at the offer. The Lord is constantly forming and molding me through my experiences. "But now, O Lord, thou art our Father; we are the clay, and thou our potter; and we all are the work of thy hand" (Isaiah 64:8).

God has been moving by opening doors for me to share His love and compassion with those in need. "I know thy works: behold, I have set before thee an open door, and no man can shut it: for thou hast a little strength, and hast kept my word, and hast not denied my name" (Revelation 3:8). God spoke to me and told me: "I pour out into you, you pour out into my people." He has also directed me in a dream to minister in the prisons. I accepted the offer from my friend to minister in the prison systems with Faith Outreach Ministries. I have sincerely thanked God for the opportunity to serve Him by ministering to His people.

For a season, I've been a member of the ministry team and have been fortunate to be a part of a group of on-fire Christian ministers. I have been given the opportunity to preach the Word, share my testimonies, pray for the sick, and sing in the prophetic. I certainly feel serving the Lord is a privilege, and being able to share Jesus with others is such a rewarding blessing. I shared my testimony on Christian radio with a dear friend and pastor, C.S. Cooley from Springfield, Massachusetts, whom I met at the prayer breakfast. I heard about a praise report from a young man in prison whose heart was touched from hearing it. I praised God for the good report. "But the Lord is faithful, who shall stablish you, and keep you from evil" (2 Thessalonians 3:3).

My family and I have visited Pastor C.S. Cooley's church and have witnessed the power and love which is truly generated from God. While in fellowship we have come to know Christians with a genuine heart, love and a burning fire for God and one another. We are so blessed to come together with other brothers and sisters in Christ. The reason the experience is so special is because the Holy Spirit has moved powerfully. The freedom and unity in the Spirit has allowed God's presence to immerse the services in His anointing. Praise God! I have always been blessed when attending fellowship there with my family.

My friends and pastors from The Master's Table Ministries, Richard and Estelle Taylor, have welcomed me and my family also with a love from the heart and hand of God. The ministry at The Master's Table consists of a Holy-Spirit-led agenda. Christ is at the forefront, and the meetings are led by the impartation and infilling from our mighty Lord and Savior Jesus Christ. God is allowed to lead the service, which enables Him to move in His unique richness, power, and glory. I have experienced a new level of praise and worship there and give all the glory to Jesus.

God is a God of faithfulness. When we come to Him with a willing and humble heart, God will recognize our needs and give to us because His promises are true. The fire of God will burn with His brilliance when we welcome Him in our lives and break away from our flesh and step into God's inner courts. We will then be filled with His presence, bondages will be broken, people will be healed and delivered. I feel it is such an honor to come into God's presence, His sweet anointing. "And it shall come to pass in that day, that his burden shall be taken away from off thy shoulder, and his yoke from off thy neck, and the yoke shall be destroyed because of the anointing" (Isaiah 10:27).

Chapter 31

Divine Appointment

I had been working on a communications system on a high-rise
rooftop and was on my way down the service elevator, stopping
at many floors on the way to ground level. As we continued to stop
and people and equipment got on and off the elevator at various
floors, a maintenance man loaded an office desk onto the elevator.
He got in, and as the door closed, he immediately turned to me and
said, "Do you want this desk?" I said, "Definitely." Then he told me
he'd help with loading it in my vehicle. My response was, "Great!"
I'm usually slow to speak but this day I was quick to accept the
offer. A particular pastor's face flashed through my mind though I
didn't even get a chance to pray about it.

As we loaded the desk into my vehicle, I found out that what
looked light actually turned out to feel like a ton. I thought, how
could a desk weigh this much. When I left the parking lot, I knew
I needed to call Pastor Cooley. As soon as I got home I called him
to ask if he needed an office desk. He thought for a moment and
said yes. I told him I'd deliver it at his church. We set up a time for
me to deliver the desk.

As I unloaded it and was getting ready to leave, the pastor
drove in. We took the drawers out of the desk and carried everything into the church and set it up in his office. After we finished,
we got together and shared our testimonies. We then started praying, and as we did it seemed as though God opened up the flood-
gates of heaven and was pouring out a blessing. The blessing was
His powerful presence. We both became so filled with the Spirit of
God. We continued to pray and then started to intercede, speaking

in tongues. We didn't know whom we were praying for, but were about to find out.

As we continued to pray, we heard a loud noise outside in the street. We rushed out the front door and realized a young girl had been hit by a car. I ran over to her to see if she was okay and found she was in minor pain. I prayed for Jesus to heal her and bring peace upon her. She told me she knew Jesus. I told her to lie still and that the pastor had run in to call an ambulance–it would be here shortly.

It wasn't long before a member of her family showed up, followed by the police department and the ambulance crew. She was strapped to a backboard and transferred to the hospital in a matter of minutes.

Sometimes we don't know what the extent of God's plan really is, but He always does have a plan. Interceding for this young girl possibly saved her life. I praise God for protecting her. "Thou art my hiding place; thou shalt preserve me from trouble; thou shall compass me about with songs of deliverance" (Psalm 32:7).

Chapter 32

911 Wake-Up Call

After the September 11, 2001 World Trade Center disaster, I spent two days at Ground Zero and four days at the Armory as a volunteer. It wasn't much time, but it left an impact on my life that I will never forget. It was one of the most unbelievable tragedies one could ever witness. Such a devastation of lives and property of enormous proportions.

I knew God allowed me to view the destruction to bring me further and deeper into a place of brokenness. He also used this experience to enlarge my passion for souls to be brought into the kingdom. My heart at this point was breaking as I felt the pain of the families who had lost their loved ones, and I felt the suffering and fear of those who had faced their violent deaths. I was in shock as I looked and couldn't believe my eyes. I was so upset I could hardly take a breath of air. I mourned and I cried and walked away in sorrow.

I didn't go to New York City to place judgment on anyone or anything, but I will say I was amazed to see so many people from all walks of life pulling together in unity. Praise God. I witnessed the extreme dedication of firefighters, police, military personnel, rescue and utility crews, medical staff, volunteers, federal agencies and branches of the city and state government workers, even down to the people cheering the crews, the supplies continually being delivered and the foods that were being prepared. I was blessed to see many ministries who were involved lending support. People were doing absolutely everything possible to proceed with the monumental task at hand. I marveled as people came together in love for their fellow man.

People have asked me, where was God on September 11, 2001? God was there. He is the one who prevented the disaster from being even more traumatic than it was. He sheltered tens of thousands of people on that day by preventing them from getting killed or disabled and prevented the destruction from taking up even more of an area. Ever since the days of Adam and Eve, when Satan opened up the doors to sin, God has never taken man's free will away from him. Our free will is a gift that God doesn't take back. We are born with it. Man's free will, though orchestrated by the armies of satanic power, is what caused those massive disasters in our country on 9/11.

Prayer is one of the keys of eliminating the attacks from the enemy. I hope and pray we as Americans will all turn to God in reverence and love of our Creator and allow God to be at the center of our lives.

We have abandoned God, put Him in a box and locked Him up. We've locked God out of our lives through the separation of church and state, which is not even found in the United States Constitution. We allow freedom concerning everything imaginable in America, but we don't allow someone their constitutional rights when it comes to freedom of speech regarding prayer and appreciation for God. Freedom of religion is one of the five rights guaranteed by our First Amendment.

The more we alienate ourselves from God, the more we are setting ourselves up for disaster. We are being stripped away from our freedom and our democracy because we are turning ourselves away from God. On America's money, the words "In God We Trust" are clearly printed. We can trust God with our money, but why not with our lives? Our hearts have hardened against the things of God, and we need to ask God for a new heart and a renewed spirit. "A new heart also will I give you, and a new spirit will I put within you: and I will take away the stony heart out of your flesh, and I will give you an heart of flesh" (Ezekiel 36:26).

All God's people need to come together in prayer, for there is great power when we are in unity with one another. "If my people, which are called by my name, shall humble themselves, and pray,

and seek my face, and turn from their wicked ways: then will I
hear from heaven, and will forgive their sin, and heal their land"
(2 Chronicles 7:14).

We need to come together and pray together for each other
and for our nation, which was founded by God. The pledge of allegiance to the American flag endorses our nation under God: "I
pledge allegiance to the flag of the United States of America, and
to the republic for which it stands, one nation under God, indivis-
ible, with liberty and justice for all."

Isn't it time we recognize God as our awesome Creator, who
died for us that we may have eternal life? "For God so loved the
world, that he gave his only begotten Son, that whosoever
believeth in him should not perish, but have everlasting life. For
God sent not his Son into the world to condemn the world; but that
the world through him might be saved" (John 3:16-17).

We took the Ten Commandments out of our schools and other
public buildings, and no matter how you look at it or try to hide
the truth, we ended up opening the doors to sin. There was a reason that God had written the Ten Commandments in stone. One
reason was so that they would be preserved. We need to focus on
God and reverence Him as our Creator and Father. Certainly we
need our families and especially our children protected by God.
God will protect us and preserve us only when we obey Him
through His teachings. He teaches us in the Bible to love one
another, which is a commandment: "A new commandment I give
unto you, That ye love one another; as I have loved you, that ye
also love one another" (John 13:34).

God directed me to pray for our president, the military, and
the leaders of the nations over the years. There is supernatural
power in prayer, and when the people of the most blessed and
prosperous country in the world come together in prayer, we will
have the cutting edge above any sin or attack from the enemy.
"Evening, and morning, and at noon, will I pray, and cry aloud: and
he shall hear my voice" (Psalm 55:17).

Chapter 33

God's Continued Faithfulness

Through the course of twelve years, Laura and I have continued to seek God's will and purpose in our lives. On many occasions we have shared the passage of scripture in Matthew 19:26, which says: "But Jesus beheld them, and said unto them, With men this is impossible; but with God all things are possible."

Out of the blue, I received a call from a friend whom I hadn't seen for many years. This was the second time we had talked in about a year. He asked me if I was interested in working on a project in Virginia. At first I didn't take him seriously but asked, "What is the project all about"? He explained and then gave me the name and number of the man to contact. When I made the phone call, I suddenly realized the opportunity was real and was able to work out all the details and necessary paperwork.

Finally after a few months, I was requested to report to work. The project, which was scheduled to take a few weeks, ended up taking many months because of additional customer requirements. Once the work in Virginia was completed, I was assigned to another project in Wisconsin, which lasted for a shorter period of time. The projects involved county-wide communications system upgrades and was directed by a top-notch company. The door of opportunity not only opened for our finances, but also Laura and Tommy were able to spend time with me and tour Washington, DC and areas of Wisconsin through the summer months.

I was happy to return home from my assignments, which took about eight months. Laura and I discussed taking some time off and traveling to Florida but we weren't making any plans until we spent time in prayer. During prayer early one morning, the Holy Spirit gave me a person's name. I didn't know what to think about it, and was trying to figure out who this person was. One week later while I was in prayer, the Lord directed me to the Internet, to check out the town of Melbourne, Florida. I was amazed to see the name of the person while reading about a revival that took place at a local church. It didn't make much sense to me, but the Lord knew what He was doing. I believed He was directing us. "For my thoughts are not your thoughts, neither are your ways my ways, saith the Lord. For as the heavens are higher than the earth, so are my ways higher than your ways, and my thoughts than your thoughts" (Isaiah 55:8-9).

For many months, my wife and I were asking the Lord if we could move so that we would be closer to my family, and asked Him for favor. "Delight thyself also in the Lord; and he shall give thee the desires of thine heart. Commit thy way unto the Lord; trust also in him; and he shall bring it to pass" (Psalm 37:4-5).

I looked on the Internet for a local realtor to make an appointment to look at apartments and new housing developments during our visit. I attempted to work out every detail to make good use of the time we had to spend during our visit to Florida.

After spending many months away from home, I needed to spend some quality time with Laura and Tommy. We were looking forward to our flight, going to the beach, checking out the area, and looking at homes.

Upon arrival at the airport we found the weather to be absolutely beautiful. During our travels we called on a person who had a for sale sign posted on their front lawn. We made an appointment to look at their house. The couple was from the Middle East and had two lovely children. I could never forget their gracious hospitality. Their home was very nice, but we were unable to work out all the details. I took the opportunity to witness with them about Jesus. I met with the man on another day to pray, read, and discuss Scripture. As a matter of fact, he had such a hunger for Jesus that I was excited to share the Gospel with Him.

After touring many developments with the aid of the realtors, we decided to seriously take another look at the first model home we looked at. We discussed the building process with the sales agent, including some changes, cost, completion, closing and move-in dates. My wife turned to me and asked, "What are you doing? We don't have all the funds and commitment letter for our mortgage." I answered by saying, "Don't you have faith? God will provide for us." "Again I say unto you, That if two of you shall agree on earth as touching any thing that they shall ask, it shall be done for them of my Father which is in heaven" (Matthew 18:16).

Our sales agent brought us through all the information and paperwork in a professional and friendly manner. Our mortgage agent, which ironically my wife found in a local newspaper, had given us a preliminary approval after completing tons of paperwork. This approval satisfied the sales agent's requirements and allowed us to continue with our plans to purchase our new home. We ended up signing all the necessary documents and paying the initial deposit. We left the office excited and believing that God would make a way. "Behold, I will do a new thing; now it shall spring forth; shall ye not know it? I will even make a way in the wilderness, and rivers in the desert" (Isaiah 43:19).

Through the years following my bankruptcy, I thought I would never be able to purchase another home. We continued to see how God's grace and mercy is more than sufficient. God had been blessing us more than we could ever imagine. "Now unto him that is able to do abundantly above all that we ask or think, according to the power that worketh in us" (Ephesians 3:20).

The next day we spent looking for an apartment to live in for four months while our home was being built. After talking with the sales agent and looking at the different apartments available, we signed the rental agreement. Our move-in date was scheduled for the 24th of December.

During our trip back home, we discussed everything that had taken place in just a few days. Now my wife was looking forward to moving after telling me prior to our trip, "No way." We all felt the peace of God and knew His hand was directing us.

Shortly after returning home from our trip, my wife cried out to the Lord in prayer and asked Him for a miracle on my birthday.

She kept it a secret, between her and the Lord. On my birthday, I received another call from my friend. This time it was concerning a project located in Florida. Once I called the supervisor and learned about the job details we both came to an agreement. I called my wife and said, "Dear, you won't believe what has happened. I was offered a position in Florida and came to an agreement with the project supervisor. He told me the work will be commencing the first or second week in January." Laura finally said to me, "Tom, I was praying for you to receive a miracle on your birthday." I was overwhelmed with joy and thankful to God for another blessing.

Time was moving quickly as we were approaching our moving date. Laura and a faithful friend did about 90 percent of all the packing. The movers loaded up their truck and brought all our belongings to a storage facility in Florida.

My flight was leaving for Wisconsin the next day. I needed to make another trip to complete a project that was delayed. My plan was to work until just a few days before Christmas and then meet Laura and Tommy at the airport in Washington, DC.

My work was completed on schedule and I was able to meet my family on time. Though I was only away for a short period, we all missed each other so much. We were all looking forward to our drive to Florida and our new home. The trip took many hours and I think our son was more patient than my wife and I. We finally arrived early in the morning and thanked God for His traveling mercies.

As soon as the rental office opened, we hurried over to the apartment complex to finalize our rental agreement. The next day the movers were going to deliver our belongings, at least we hoped so. They never explained the fact that payment by check was not permissible. When they picked up our furniture back home, they told us that a personal check would be fine. It took a few hours to correct the problem with my bank, but now we were all set. They finally showed up and in a matter of hours we were moved into our new home. About a week later we finally had our home in order.

We spent our first Christmas in Florida. It was a wonderful time of year to spend celebrating the birthday of Jesus with our family.

After living in Florida for three months and traveling home on weekends, my wife gave me the second major surprise of my life. My first surprise had been when she informed me that she was pregnant with Tommy. It was my understanding from our discussions that Laura had a slim possibility of ever having a child. The second surprise was when my wife told me she was pregnant with Samuel. For close to thirteen years my wife couldn't get pregnant. Tommy was constantly saying to me, "Dad, I really want a brother." My answer to Him was, "Pray for a brother and wait and see what God does. He did pray and he received his request. "And I say unto you, Ask, and it shall be given you; seek, and ye shall find; knock, and it shall be opened unto you" (Luke 11:9).

My wife's pregnancy was a miracle and also a season of testing and trials. For the next eight months she suffered with almost daily nausea, vomiting, and gallbladder attacks. She had just started a new job, which she loved, and it was going very well, but she had to give it up. I think we lost track of the number of visits to the emergency room. She was so uncomfortable, the pain at times was unbearable. My heart really went out to her. At the eighth month she started bleeding internally and was rushed to the hospital by her friends. That same evening I was contemplating coming home, but I was tired and decided to spend the night and drive home in the morning. I received a call from her friend and was told Laura was in the emergency room.

At the time I was hours away from home and knew I needed to rush to the hospital. I thanked our friend and told her I was on my way and asked if she would inform me of any complications. After driving for a while, it felt like I would never get there. I found myself almost falling asleep. The Lord sustained Laura, Samuel, and me. At this point I knew the Lord had a good reason for me to drive at this given time. He predestined this time for me to pray and offer up all my family's needs to Him. I've learned an important key to spiritual growth with God, which is to fully trust Him.

Upon finally reaching the hospital, I was told my wife had given birth to our son Samuel during an emergency C-section and that he was healthy. Praise the Lord! Though I wasn't able to witness his birth, our dear friend graciously took my place. I was disappointed but happy everything was under control. When I finally got a chance to see our little baby boy, I noticed he looked as beautiful and precious as Tommy did when he was born. Tommy was thrilled to see his dear brother too and has been a big help taking care of him. Samuel admires Tommy even at a young age.

Since Samuel was born five weeks early, he had to be transferred to another hospital that had the facilities to care for him. The hardest of our eight-month ordeal was when he was taken by an ambulance to another hospital. We knew he was in good hands because the doctors, nurses, and ambulance personnel were the best. We were impressed and very pleased with their excellent care, compassion, and professionalism.

Samuel was connected to various life support systems along with every monitor you could imagine. We knew he was in the best possible place, but it was still difficult for us to see him in this condition. We were surprised and happy when he was allowed to come home one week later. It was great bringing him home with all of us. We received a call from his doctor a couple of days later. He explained that because Samuel was born prematurely, some of his blood levels didn't appear to be normal. He told us we needed to take Samuel to have some blood work done. Many people spent many hours in prayer believing God would intervene. At first the readings were not normal, but we kept taking him to have his blood checked. Finally we received word that his blood levels were fine. With Samuel home and my wife feeling a little better, we started getting on track.

One week after Laura gave birth, she ended up back in the hospital to have her gallbladder removed. She was in extreme pain and was rushed to the hospital. The doctor ordered an emergency operation. Thank God the operation was a success and soon she would be back to normal. She ended up spending two days in the hospital and finally was sent home. It was a joy to have her home once again.

While traveling throughout the state of Florida, I have had the opportunity to minister. I have witnessed cancer healed, bondages broken and lives restored through the healing power of Jesus. "For I will restore health unto thee, and I will heal thee of thy wounds, saith the Lord" (Exodus 15:26).

The other day I prayed with a father, mother, and little girl that were in an automobile accident. Apparently the man took his eyes off the road for a few seconds and ended up losing control. His car spun in circles across the highway and ended up in a ditch twenty feet off the road. No one even had a scratch.

"Great is our Lord, and of great power" (Psalm 147:5a).

Chapter 34

Invitation to Receive
Jesus as Your Savior

God has brought me to a place of understanding regarding all His divine interventions in my life, which I have shared throughout this book. The question remains: "Why did God spare my life?" I realized each hurting circumstance, including the trials, temptations, and tribulations, were the catalysts God used to bring me to an understanding that unless I suffered, I could not be used for God's purpose in my life. "Then said Jesus unto his disciples, If any man will come after me, let him deny himself, and take up his cross, and follow me. For whosoever will save his life shall lose it: and whosoever will lose his life for my sake shall find it" (Matthew 16:24-25).

God has taught me to be an overcomer, so that I may partake of His divine purpose, which He ordained before my birth. "To him that overcometh will I give to eat of the tree of life, which is in the midst of the paradise of God" (Revelation 2:7b). We are birthed for a divine purpose in Christ Jesus through His resurrection to glorify Him and seek His will in our lives. During worship service recently at church God spoke to me, "Everything you do, do it for My Glory."

The following scripture relates to our walk with Him. "Who hath saved us, and called us with a holy calling, not according to our works, but according to his own purpose and grace, which was given us in Christ Jesus before the world began" (2 Timothy 1:9). Have you found your God-given purpose yet?

Please pray with me:

Heavenly Father, we recognize you're leading through your written and spoken word. Please make yourself known to me so I may fulfill my destiny and purpose in my life. I long to be free from desperate needs and demands on my life. Prepare my heart, Lord, to receive you as my Lord and Savior.

For whosoever shall call upon the name of the Lord shall be saved (Romans 10:13).

I believe in Jesus Christ for he is the Son of God (1 John 5:13).

I believe Jesus Christ died on the cross for the forgiveness of my sins through the shedding of his blood (1Peter 2:24) (Ephesians 1:7).

I confess I am a sinner (Romans 3:23).

I ask for forgiveness for all my sins (1John 1:9).

I confess that Jesus is the Lord over my life and I believe God raised Jesus from the dead (Romans 10:9).

I ask you, Jesus, to come into my heart and become my personal Savior,

In Jesus' precious name, Amen.

"In my Father's house are many mansions: if it were not so, I would have told you. I go to prepare a place for you" (John 14:2). God has prepared a beautiful and magnificent place for you to spend eternity with Him. "EYE HATH NOT SEEN, NOR EAR HEARD, NEITHER HAVE ENTERED INTO THE HEART OF MAN, THE THINGS WHICH GOD HATH PREPARED FOR THEM THAT LOVE HIM" (1 Corinthians 2:9).

For prayer requests, please contact:

Impacting Lives Ministries International
PO Box 881771
Port St. Lucie, FL 34988-1771
E-mail address: Impactinglvs@aol.com
Phone: 561-674-7783

You Have a Purpose
Order Form

Telephone orders: 561-674-7783

E-mail orders: Impactinglvs@aol.com

Mail orders: Impacting Lives Ministries International
PO Box 881771
Port St. Lucie, FL 34988-1771

Please send *You Have a Purpose* to:

Name: _____

Address: _____

City: _____ State: _____

Zip: _____

Telephone: (_____) _____

Book Price: $12.95

Shipping: $3.00 for the first book and $1.00 for each additional book to cover shipping and handling within US, Canada, and Mexico. International orders add $6.00 for the first book and $2.00 for each additional book.

Or order from:
ACW Press
P.O. Box 110390
Nashville, TN 37222

(800) 931-BOOK

or contact your local bookstore